Not Much Longer NOW

Tragedy, Murder Headlines, and the Hope of Heaven

Julie Wheeler Mayfield

ISBN 978-1-68526-256-3 (Paperback)
ISBN 978-1-68526-257-0 (Digital)

Covenant Books
11661 Hwy 707
Murrells Inlet, SC 29576
www.covenantbooks.com

For Will, who believes God

Contents

Foreword

Sometimes leaning into the hard edges of life softens the rest of the journey, and taking a bitter pill can give a sweetness to the remainder of the banquet that the Lord has prepared for us. This book gives us excellent examples of those experiences. With the turning of each page we are able to see how the Lord's presence lifts this family from the depths of despair to those holy moments of miracles and strength that only the Lord can give at just the right time and in just the right dose. You, the reader, will be blessed by sharing this journey with this special family as they share those very personal experiences and moments with you. You will walk away a better person for having done so.

Many blessings.

In His service,
Dr. Reggie Anderson
Author of *Appointments with Heaven*

Acknowledgments

To Will, the steadiest husband a woman could ask for. You truly do still believe God, even after suffering such unimaginable pain and loss; you spur me on every day to do the same. That you would marry me and stay with me all these years in spite of my many flaws is the most tangible picture I have of the gospel. Thank you for your constant encouragement to write, and for entrusting me with your story.

To our children, Emily, William, Luke, and Caleb. These tragedies occurred during your most formative years. I am so sorry. And I am so sorry that my preoccupation with grief and my depression kept me from being as engaged and present with you as I should have been during those years. Thank you for loving me anyway. God has used what we have walked through to grow such compassionate hearts within you. I am so thankful for the evidence of this I see in your lives. Boys, may God continue to grow you into men of integrity. Emily, you have been my greatest cheerleader throughout this writing process. I don't have adequate words to express how much that has meant to me. You have put in many hours editing my work along the way, and I am so grateful. What a gift to have my young adult daughter become my friend!

To Dad. You showed us that "in sickness and in health" is not an empty phrase; it is love in action. We were watching. Your grandchildren were watching. You watched your lovely wife suffer immensely, and you leaned in and cared for her, enduring sleepless nights and exhausting days. Thank you for faithfully journaling for those ten years and for sharing it with us all; credit goes to you for much of the information I've included surrounding the details of Mom's years as a quadriplegic.

To Mom's caregivers. Taking care of a ventilator-dependent quadriplegic is both physically and emotionally challenging. There were many of you, and we saw every act of service and love you did for Mom, as well as for our whole family. You put up with a lot when we were all around; screaming babies crawling and running around in your workspace, family tension, change in your routines. But we also shared a lot of joy together, and you are forever an extension of our family. We love you all.

To Covenant Presbyterian Church in Cleveland, MS, for raising money for an accessible van for Mom.

To Covenant Presbyterian Church in Fayetteville, GA. You all were on the frontlines for our family; volunteer caregivers, construction to make the house accessible, meals, financial help, faithful friends, the list could go on and on.

To Christ Presbyterian Church in Nashville, TN. You have expanded our view of disability ministry.

To our connect group. We didn't form until after these tragedies, but it is a joy to learn and walk together and to pray for one another.

To my Tuesday morning Bible-study small group ladies, you surrounded me with prayer, friendship, and empathy. I love you all.

To Karen and Reggie Anderson. Karen, I honestly don't know where I would be today without you. Thank you for walking faithfully with me and for always reminding me of the truth. The love of Jesus spills out of you. Reggie, thank you for writing your story; it truly encouraged me and gave me hope when my days were so dark.

To Covenant Presbyterian Church in Jackson, MS. You suffered a tremendous shock and loss as well, along with Mom and Dad Mayfield's whole community. You fed us, ministered to us, and grieved alongside us.

To Will's partners and the staff of Premier and Hughston Clinic Orthopaedics and Stonecrest Hospital. Thank you for your dedication to providing the highest level of patient care and for supporting Will so that he can do the same. Thank you for caring for his patients when these tragedies occurred.

To the first responders, nurses, and physicians whose kind hands cared for my mom and Will's parents. We never even met many of you, but thank you.

To Dad Mayfield's attorney, Cynthia Speetjens. We are forever grateful for your defense and for eventually having Dad's record expunged.

To my counselor, Margaret Phillips. I am so grateful for your counsel and compassion, which slowly drew me up out of the dark hole of depression.

To Catha Skinner. Thank you for encouraging me to write this book and for cheering for me along the way.

To Joni and Friends. You have made an indelible print on our family forever, and we are grateful.

In loving memory of Bill and Susan Mayfield, who welcomed me and treated me as a daughter when I married their son.

And in loving memory of my mom, Lynn Wheeler, who in spite of her immense suffering continued to believe "whatever my God ordains is right."

Introduction

Maybe you *can* go back again. I recently took a trip down memory lane. I had never intended to go back, but early in the summer of 2019, I did. It started with a hotel reservation south of Atlanta to break up a long road trip with my eldest, Emily, and youngest, Caleb. Our plans also included dinner to catch up with two precious friends. A tragedy at the end of 2005 brought them into our lives. Otherwise, we likely would have never met.

We had a wonderful visit telling old stories and sharing what was going on in our lives. We laughed and we cried. Two hours was not long enough with Liz and Kristy. I could have spent days sharing memories with them.

After dinner, I mentioned that I would like to drive by the house, so Liz rode with us and directed me there. This was Mom and Dad's house when a job change brought them to Atlanta in 2003. We had made some wonderful memories with my extended family here. Our babies, their grandchildren, were tiny, and some were still to be born when they first moved into this house. Baby toys, dolls, and cars were strewn all over the floors of the house whenever we visited, but Mom and Dad did not mind. In fact, they loved it! Dad chased the kids around the house, and Mom played with them on the floor. The walls of that house were filled with baby giggles, music, and stories being read aloud.

I stopped the car in front of the house, snapped a picture, and gazed at the house and the backyard for a moment, remembering. My mind was flooded with sweet memories of Dad telling scary stories around the firepit out back as the grandchildren squealed with delight. As I looked at the living room window, I remembered Mom going around the house opening all the blinds to let the light in on that Christmas morning so long ago.

For a few moments, I fixed my gaze on the driveway, the place I had watched my mom take her final steps on this earth. I glanced at the renovations that had to be done to the house after that day: the front porch with a concrete ramp, the accessible deck out back, and the wider front door that had been added. It was surprising to me that the house pretty much looked the same. I had expected to be overwhelmed with sadness looking at their house, but instead there was a great peace. It was a sweet surprise, and then I realized this: I never expect God to surprise me.

We had stopped that evening at the Marble Slab, where Mom and Dad had occasionally spoiled the grandchildren with ice cream when we visited, and we had breakfast the next morning at the Truett's, where we had shared meals together.

On our way out of town, we stopped by the second house my parents had lived in while in the Atlanta area. The kids remembered the zipline that Dad had installed for them out back, and they remembered spending hours riding their scooters down the long ramp in the front of the house. Again, I expected a flood of great sadness, but instead there was peace.

God gave me the gift of some healing during that short visit. As I sat looking at the houses and remembering, it seemed like a lifetime ago that my parents were there. The trauma of what happened on December 25, 2005, has weighed on me every day since it happened. But now, over fourteen years later, that trauma finally feels as though it is mostly in the past.

The houses I went back to visit were still there. I thought about the fact that their foundations were still holding them up, and I realized that my foundation has held me secure as well. There have been times over the years that I thought I had been blown away from my foundation, but my foundation is Jesus, and he has held me.

I always thought the tragedy that happened that day would be all that God would send, but years down the road, there would come another unthinkable event involving my husband Will's family. I had no idea that we would lose three parents in their sixties, all through separate tragedies. They were all the picture of health and of lives lived out through faith in Jesus.

This is the story of my life together with Will's as it has been written so far: of joys and sorrows, celebrations and sufferings. But this is really the story of a God who is faithful and carries his people through life in spite of our weakness and unfaithfulness. It is also a story of hope restored: Not the hope of our circumstances improving and us returning to a comfortable life, but the hope in our resurrected Jesus, who promised that he would come again and make all things new. Tragedy has given me a longing for heaven that I never had before these events, so that I can now say with the psalmist, "How lovely is your dwelling place, O Lord of hosts! My soul longs, yes, faints for the courts of the Lord; my heart and flesh sing for joy to the living God" (Psalm 84:1–2 ESV).

I know we do not have a corner on suffering. Many of you reading this book have been or are currently in the storms of your lives. If you have not yet experienced suffering, you will. Jesus himself said, "In this world you will have trouble. But take heart! I have overcome the world" (John 16:33 NIV).

Over the past few years, I have wondered how we should steward our story. I have prayed about it on and off. In June of 2018, a dear friend approached me about writing a book. I laughed it off at first, but she said she was serious. After much prayer and deliberation, I began to write. As the book evolved, I determined the reasoning behind writing it is threefold.

First, this is the story of a God who is faithful to preserve his children through trials and suffering. It is not about my faith. As you will read in these pages, I have doubted, questioned, and wrestled with God. I have also spent ten long years being angry at him. So if you are looking to read about someone who, when faced with tragedy, immediately responded by trusting God and saying that all things work together for good, you have picked up the wrong book. I know people who have been given that gift of faith and who trust very quickly; that is a beautiful gift from God. However, for many years of this journey, I have been like the toddler who, when her daddy holds her in his arms trying to console her, arches her back, wanting to be put down. However, God has not let me down; he has held me the whole time. Instead of letting me go, he gave me a long wrestling match with him, and I am grateful that he emerged victorious as he always does. Although I emerged with a limp, I am thankful for the limp because it reminds me of his faithfulness.

Second, my desire is that this story will be a defense of my hope. First Peter 3:15 says, "But in your hearts honor Christ the Lord as holy, always being prepared to make a defense to anyone who asks you for a reason for the hope that is in you; yet do it with gentleness and respect…" (ESV). I do have hope, and I hope that as you read, it will be clear that my hope does not lie in my circumstances or in things going well for me. It rests in my Lord and Savior Jesus Christ, who took on flesh and came to suffer and die for me. While the Lord's hold on me has never wavered, my hope is in constant flux. Sometimes it is a rich, robust hope, and other times it barely dangles by a thread. The object of my hope, however, never changes.

I want to share hope with readers who have suffered traumatic losses or who have endured suffering of any kind. As we share our stories, we become more aware of the hurt that others carry; we gain a whole new kind of empathy. Shared stories let us know that we are not alone; everyone we meet has faced or will face suffering. One of the most helpful tools for me in the midst of our grief was reading books in which Christians shared their stories of suffering. I read several, but there were two that really stood out to me and encouraged me. *Appointments with Heaven*, written by our friend Reggie Anderson, was full of real struggle and loss and overwhelming hope. It was a beautiful picture to me of just how thin the veil is between here and eternity. The other book, *Set Free*, was written by Stephen Owens, a science teacher at our children's school. He writes about the murder of his father, and about how God is able to bring us to a place of being able to forgive.

Third and finally, I am writing because I do not want the suffering of our parents to be wasted. I am writing to give them a voice because I know their desire would be to point each of you to Jesus as your ultimate hope. All of them trusted in Jesus as their Lord and Savior. They are no longer exercising faith and hope, but they are in heaven in the presence of Jesus. Their faith has become sight, and their hope has been fulfilled. Hebrews 11:1 (NIV) says, "Now faith is being sure of what we hope for and certain of what we do not see."

Because the tragedy involving Will's parents was so public, I believe it is important that their hope is shared publicly. They would have wanted nothing more than for others to hear about their hope in Jesus. My mother would want the same.

I also want to clarify why my account of my mother's suffering is so much longer than that of Will's parents. It has nothing to do with importance and everything to do with the time that elapsed from beginning to end. My mother's journey of tragedy and suffering extended over a ten-year period, while that of Will's parents spanned a mere five weeks.

Even though she is no longer with us, my beautiful mother-in-law, Susan Mayfield, gave me the title for this book. I was recently sorting through some of my mother's things when I came across a note attached to a piece of paper. It was a short, handwritten note from Will's mother to my mother, and it simply stated, "Lynn, Bill and I thought you might enjoy this. Not much longer now! Love, S." Attached to it was a short devotional, dated September 12, 1999, just eleven days before our first child, their first grandchild, was born. It was entitled, "Godly Grandmothers," and at the very end it listed three tips for grandmothers. "Pray for your grandchildren. Play with your grandchildren. Pass on your faith to your grandchildren." They both did all three of these.

I know that her words, "Not much longer now," meant that it was almost time to welcome their first grandchild. It was an arrival that they had been anticipating for quite a while, and they were all so excited. But when I stumbled upon this note and read the words for the first time recently, my mind immediately went to another arrival that I am eagerly anticipating. In Revelation 22:20, Jesus says, "Surely I am coming soon" (ESV). When Jesus comes back, he will make all things new. The promise that he is coming soon gives me not only hope for eternity but also the ability to continue to live with hope each day. It is not much longer now!

Before this story begins, I want to be clear about something. It is not easy to hear, but it is true. There are many who believe that heaven is just a place everyone goes when they die. Others believe that it is a place for everyone who has lived a good life, whose good deeds outweigh their bad.

Only one lived a good life, a perfect life, and that was Jesus. He lived a perfect life, fulfilling the law on our behalf. Then he suffered and died a horrific death in the place of his children. He was resurrected three days later, conquering death and securing eternal life for us through him. In John 14:6, Jesus says about himself, "I am the way, and the truth, and the life. No one comes to the Father except through me" (ESV).

Our pastor at Christ Presbyterian Church, Scott Sauls, often says this at the end of the sermon, referring to the hope he has preached: "This hope is only for those who are resting in Jesus for their salvation. If that does not describe you, then I'm sorry, but I have no hope for you." This may be painful to hear, and it may sound harsh, but according to the Bible, it is true and loving. Hope in anything or anyone other than Jesus will only disappoint and will lead to death. Scott always follows his statement with, "Anyone can get in on this!"

Chapter 1

Things Would Never Be the Same

December 25, 2005

It was a dreary, wet morning as our caravan set out for church that Sunday: Mom was in the vehicle ahead of us with my brother Jeff's family, and Dad was in our car with my family.

We were only a few minutes from their home when I looked up and saw a tire rolling toward us. As we rounded the bend in the road, I heard Dad yell, "Oh God, is that Jeff's truck in the ditch?" My husband, Will, pulled over, quickly parking in the grass. He and Dad ran to the scene.

Disbelief. Shock. The sensation of being an outsider observing the chaos unfolding around me. Suddenly I was jarred back to reality by the sound of screaming babies in the car with me. A broken record in my head playing, "Oh God, this isn't happening, this isn't happening!"

*****

Will and I knew we were blessed with our extended families. They were certainly not perfect, but we enjoyed the times we could all be together. We alternated holidays with our families, and we enjoyed all the fun and chaos that came with lots of little cousins being together. It was such a joy seeing our parents loving their roles as grandparents, and they were very involved in all of our lives.

Christmas of 2005 was the year for my side of the family to be together at my parents' house outside Atlanta. We were thrilled to be together and to celebrate Mom being cancer free, following the past ten months of surgery and treatment.

On a walk together a day or two before Christmas, Mom told my sister-in-law Wendy that she felt like God had given her the cancer to prepare her for something else. She felt like something more was ahead.

Because Christmas fell on a Sunday that year, we celebrated our big Christmas morning the day before, on Saturday. It was a wonderful morning, the children ripping open gifts and squealing with delight, the living room floor covered in wrapping paper and boxes. Mom went around opening the blinds, as she had always loved the outdoors and natural light. Then we had a sweet time of Gram (the name my children had given my mom) leading her little grandchildren in acting out the nativity.

We went to the Christmas Eve service at their church and then came home and attempted to get a nice picture of Mom and Dad with the five grandchildren, who were six years old and younger. Needless to say, the babies weren't up for the occasion. The picture shows two laughing grandparents holding two mad babies and a red balloon!

After dinner, Gram brought out a birthday cake for Jesus, a new tradition she wanted to start with her grandchildren. The children all gathered around the kitchen table, Mom lit the candles, and we all sang "Happy Birthday" to Jesus. I snapped a picture, capturing little faces full of wonder.

Christmas morning was full of the typical craziness of trying to get little ones out the door for church. My sister Susan and her husband, Todd, left early to drive to Mobile to spend Christmas with Todd's family. Mom had prepared Sunday lunch, put it in the oven, and set the timer for it to cook while we were at church. I remember insisting on getting a picture of the cousins, and someone else was busy plunging a toilet. A few minutes later, I watched Mom come outside and jump into the back seat of Jeff's car so she could sit between his children, Madison and Nelson. They pulled out of the driveway, and then Dad came out of the house and got into the van with our family.

A few minutes later, we arrived at the horrific accident scene. A teenage boy had lost control coming around a curve, hitting my brother's SUV head-on and sending both cars off the road and into a ditch.

The next thing I remember was Jeff running back to the van, handing me his phone, and yelling for me to call the church. Through sobs, he told me that Will was working on Mom; she was not breathing. Several cars had already stopped, and someone called 911. I waited for someone at the church to answer the phone, and finally Pastor Dale answered. I told him there had been an accident and that Mom was in bad shape.

Jeff got his kids out of the car and brought them back to me in the van. Maddie got into the car and was able to walk around, but when I put Nelson down, he refused to stand. Then I saw Jeff struggle to get the front passenger door of his car open so that he could get Wendy out. I remember seeing her fall onto the ground. Jeff checked on her, and then I remember seeing a woman come and kneel beside her and hold her hand. I stretched my arms out in an attempt to keep the children from seeing what was going on outside. My six-year-old daughter Emily kept whispering from the back, "I'm hungry, Mommy." William, my four-year-old, sat quietly in his seat.

I was somewhat in shock watching the scene unfold, and I was having trouble taking care of the five young children in the car with me. Nelson, eighteen months old, and my son Luke, fourteen months old, were screaming. I could not console them. Then the van door opened to reveal a woman around Mom's age and her daughter asking if they could help. They each took a screaming baby boy and carried them, pacing up and down the road, trying to comfort them. Frozen in my seat from the shock, I looked up to see an ambulance, and leaning up against it, my sobbing brother, in the solid embrace of a large African American man. We later learned that he was a pastor on the way to his own church to preach the Christmas morning message.

I saw Wendy loaded onto a stretcher and then into an ambulance. Will came walking back to the car. There was a little blood on his shirt. He had given Mom rescue breathing until the ambulance arrived. Her pulse was very faint. The paramedics had intubated her, and Dad rode with her in the ambulance. Because of how the cars were positioned, the kids and I were unable to see Will working on Mom. I was very grateful that the children had not witnessed this.

Will drove me, Jeff, and the five children back to the house to drop me off with our three children. The ambulance had rushed Mom to the nearest hospital, and then the paramedics brought Dad back to the house. Mom was going to be Life-Flighted to downtown Atlanta, and Dad wasn't allowed to fly with her. He said that Mom's heart had stopped twice on the way to the local hospital.

Will took Jeff, Madison, and Nelson to Grady Hospital, where Wendy had been taken, so that they could be examined in the emergency room. He took Dad to Atlanta Medical Center, where Mom had been Life-Flighted. There, she underwent emergency surgery for life-threatening injuries sustained in the accident.

Walking into the house with our three children was one of the loneliest times of my life. I remember heading straight for the oven to remove the food that Mom had prepared for Christmas dinner. I called Susan to tell her about the accident, and to tell her that we did not know if Mom would live. Susan and Todd were already several hours down the road to Mobile by this point, but they turned around to head back to Atlanta. Shock and denial had already set in, along with the desire to turn back the clock an hour. I called my friend Christie back home to tell her, and she passed the news along to our pastor, who called me soon after hearing the news from her.

I was frustrated, struggling to take care of my young children, who were very afraid and confused by what had transpired. I remember talking to a friend of Mom and Dad's from church who called to let me know she was in surgery. He had no idea what was wrong with her, except that the surgery was emergent. I called him several times over the next few hours, pressing him, begging for some news, but he had none.

The rest of that afternoon was a blur, taking care of children, praying, crying out to God, wondering if Mom would live, and really needing some help. Late that afternoon, there was a knock on the door. I opened it, and there stood Jeff and Catha Skinner, whom I did not know well, but I remember they looked like angels to me. They had just recently moved to the Nashville area from Atlanta, and they had come back home to spend Christmas with family and friends. They had been at Mom and Dad's church that morning, where they heard the news of the accident. I think I remember Jeff serving the kids some ice cream and playing with them.

They told me about how the accident had changed the church service that morning. When I called the church from the accident scene, hoping someone would answer, it was almost time for the service to start. Normally, the pastor's office would have been empty at that time, but Pastor Dale was there and picked up the phone. In the service, they announced that there had been a terrible accident and that Mom was severely injured and not breathing. They had a special time of prayer.

At some point, Will arrived home with three-year-old Madison, who had been checked out at the hospital and seemed to be fine. I felt like I needed to do something normal, so I figured I should bathe the kids. I think Catha helped me. Sweet Maddie cried the whole time in the tub, and I realized why when I saw all the bruising from her car seat restraints. Soon Jeff, Wendy, and Nelson arrived home with no severe injuries, praise God. They all had trauma and bruising from seat belts and airbags. Jeff seemed to have an injured leg, Nelson still would not walk on his injured leg, and Wendy's physical injuries seemed the most pronounced. Dad came home at some point to try to sleep, and he told us that Mom was in the ICU following emergency abdominal surgery to stop internal bleeding.

That night, I listened to Will describe the accident scene. He said that when he first looked into the car and saw Mom, her head was slumped over. Just before she lost consciousness, she looked at him and mouthed to him, "I can't breathe." He said he told her, "It's okay, I'll breathe for you." Because Mom was seated in the middle of the car between two car seats, Will knew he had to get her out of the car in order to have room to work on her. He also was unsure of the risk of her remaining in the car, as there was either steam or smoke pouring from the engine. Being a physician and aware of the possibility of traumatic injury, he helped Dad remove her very carefully from the car and laid her on the ground. She was not breathing, and she had a very weak pulse. Will administered rescue breathing until the ambulance arrived.

I do not think any of us really slept well that night. I know I did not. I remember waking multiple times in the night, crying, praying, and talking to Will. We had traveled in two cars because he was supposed to leave late on Christmas Day and drive home to get back to work and take call, while the kids and I had planned to stay a few more days. After the accident, Will called one of his partners at work, and he and others were able to work out coverage for call so that Will could be with us one more day.

We were finally able to visit Mom the morning after the accident. She was in the ICU with many tubes coming out of her and going into machines. As a result of her abdominal injuries, the surgeon performed a colostomy, removing a good bit of her colon. Mom had an ostomy bag, which was possibly temporary. She was on a ventilator, was still wearing the cervical collar, and could not feel her arms and legs. Because of the ventilator, she was unable to talk, but she was wide awake and mouthing words to us. She was smiling and even joking with one of the church officers who was there with us about making him some really strong coffee.

In spite of her critical condition, Mom asked about Jeff's family, wanting to be sure they were safe, and she was so relieved and thankful when we told her they were going to be all right. The "momma bear" protective instinct is so strong and fierce. Mom's right arm was bruised and swollen. Nelson had been seated to her right, and his car seat had shifted upon impact. More than likely, when she realized they were going to crash, Mom had flung her arms in front of Nelson and Maddie in order to protect them.

There is a denial that sets in in situations like this. Things do not seem real. I felt as though time had stopped. We were in the middle of a nightmare. I remember thinking that Mom would be fine, that she would start breathing on her own and moving her limbs again. But I also remember weeping as I stood over her and looking across her hospital bed at Will, knowing something was terribly wrong. Since she was in the ICU, visits were brief, and we spent a good bit of time sitting in the waiting room. We went back to the house to watch the children so that Jeff and Wendy could see Mom, and then later that afternoon, Will had to leave for Nashville.

On December 27, forty-eight hours post-accident, we were finally told the full extent of her injuries. Mom had sustained a spinal cord injury that was the highest and worst possible, a C1-C2 injury. The surgeon explained that this would obviously affect movement and would also leave her unable to breathe on her own. He did leave room for hope, saying that things could possibly change once swelling went down, but that was unlikely. She had also suffered a minor head injury from the impact.

Each time I went in to see Mom lying there in that bed, all I could do was hug and kiss her and weep. We had coached swimming together, she had been my first running partner, she had held my babies and had run around the house laughing and playing with them, and now all she could do was lie in bed while a machine gave her every breath. It was not fair, and I cried out to God to do something about this.

Later that evening, I remember Dad coming home to try to sleep for the night, and he said, "I have got to find a way to bring her home to take care of her. I can't send her to live in a nursing home." Even though we did not yet understand the scope of what her needs would be, I remember wondering how in the world it would be possible to have her live at home.

The next few days were spent in much the same way, taking turns taking care of the children so the adults could visit Mom. I do not remember many details, but I know members of my parents' church fed us, spent time with us at the house, and visited Mom in the hospital. My precious friend and roommate from my time in Jackson, Laura, now lived in Atlanta, and she came to sit with us.

Before the new year, it was time for all of us to go home. I hated to leave Mom and Dad, but I needed to be with Will. I did not want him to be alone for too long after what he had been through at the accident scene, and we needed to process together.

*****

They say lightning never strikes twice in the same place. For some reason, I had unconsciously applied this to tragedy as well, reasoning that surely it would never strike twice in the same family. I was wrong.

Chapter 2

The Phone Rings

April 30, 2014

The kids were settled in bed, the house was quiet and peaceful, and I was headed to bed when the phone rang at ten that Wednesday night.

Seeing that it was my sister-in-law, Tanya, I answered it. Through the sobs on the other end, I was able to make out words I never thought I would hear. "Julie, it's Tanya. Mom's been shot, and they think Dad was the shooter!"

Her husband Nick, Will's brother, had received a call from the Jackson Police Department, and Dad was in custody. The police would not disclose anything about Mom's condition to him.

Disbelief and shock set in. I felt myself start to sob. My knees were weak, I felt nauseous, and I leaned on the kitchen counter for support.

Questions began swirling in my mind. *You have already given us such heartache. How could you do this to us again, God? Not again, God, we can't do this again. Not another tragedy.*

*****

On Monday evening, April 28, 2014, forty-eight hours before receiving that devastating phone call, I saw on the news that there were tornadoes in the Jackson, Mississippi, area. Will's parents lived there. Will rarely travels for work; maybe once a year for a conference. That evening, though, he was on a plane to go to a hospital leadership meeting in Houston. The kids were in bed, so I called Mom Mayfield around nine to make sure they were safe.

She answered immediately, and I told her I was concerned about them possibly being in the path of the tornadoes. Mom sounded very flustered, which was not at all typical for her. In fact, I had always known her to be a very composed Southern belle. I had never heard her this upset in the eighteen years I had known her.

She said, "Oh, Julie, we are okay in the storm, but I don't know how to tell you this. I guess since I've got you on the phone, I'm going to have to tell you. I am out driving around looking for Bill. He walked away from the house about an hour ago, and I can't find him. He said he wanted to watch a movie. I walked over to the cabinet to pick out a movie, and then I heard the back door close, and he was gone."

I was completely surprised by this. Will and I had no idea that she had been dealing with anything like this with Dad. I asked her if she was alone looking for him. She said she was. I asked her if she had called a friend or someone from church to help her look for him. She said she hadn't, but that she had called his neurologist. They needed to adjust his Parkinson's medications since they were causing terrible side effects. She said, "Oh, Julie, I'm afraid this is the end of our life as we know it."

Upon hanging up the phone, I prayed, and then I emailed my Tuesday morning Bible study small group to ask them to pray. I could not talk to Will since his flight hadn't yet landed, so I texted him and left him a voice mail. I called my sister-in-law, Tanya, Nick's wife, to let her know what was going on. She said that Mom mentioned Dad wandering away from the house sometime the week before.

I ended the call with Tanya and tried to call Mom several times, but she did not answer. About half an hour later, Tanya called to say she had been able to reach Mom. She had found Dad, and he was safe. He was sitting with a neighbor on the neighbor's porch.

The next morning, Tuesday, I called Mom to check on them. She was very upbeat, saying that they were fine and that Dad was really sorry for last night. She also said that they were very grateful that their neighbor hadn't called the police. He had already been to his morning men's Bible study, and her art teacher was due to arrive soon for their weekly art lesson. She then told me, "I asked Bill if he would stay downstairs during my lesson and not do anything crazy, and he said he would."

Then she began to explain to me what had happened the night before. She said, "Julie, I was so worried that Bill was lost and didn't know what he was doing. But he knew exactly what he was doing. He thought he saw bad guys at our house, so he ran outside and hid behind the bushes to watch the house." I tried to push back on this, saying that this was extremely concerning. But she said that as soon as her lesson was over, they were immediately heading to see his neurologist to adjust his medications. She said that these hallucinations were side effects of his medications and that he would be fine if they could just find the right dosages.

Will and his brothers, Nick and Alex, were in communication with Mom that day and into Wednesday about the appointment with the neurologist and Dad's medications. There were no clear answers, but she was very hopeful to see improvement with the medication adjustments.

*****

When I received the phone call about the shooting on Wednesday night, Will was on a plane home from Houston, not due to land until around eleven. I called and left a voice mail on his phone. All I could think of was that I needed help. I sent an email to my Bible study small group, and then I called Catha. She immediately came over and sat with me until Will got home.

Will had talked to his brothers on the drive home from the airport. Alex lived outside Baton Rouge at the time and was on the way to Jackson. Nick began the drive from Columbus, Georgia, which would take all night. Will decided to wait until the morning to leave.

We climbed into bed, hoping Will could maybe get a bit of sleep before the long drive to Jackson in the morning. All we knew was that Mom was in surgery at the University of Mississippi Medical Center. Alex was in the waiting room with some of Mom and Dad's closest friends. Finally, around 2:00 a.m., we got the call from Alex that Mom did not make it.

I reached over and put my arms around Will, and we cried. My mind just kept saying, *No, no, no...* And then I said no to God. *No, God, you can't take Will's beautiful mother like this.*

I wonder if this is normal when sudden, traumatic moments occur, but my response in the moment was the need to time travel. We needed to go back, to set the clock back to nine thirty last night. Everything was all right then. We just needed to go back. Maybe this is part of the denial and unbelief that sets in.

We tried to sleep, tossing and turning all night. At some point, I got up and called my sisters-in-law, Jenny and Tanya, just to talk. I knew they were alone since their husbands had left for Jackson the night before.

The next morning was awful. Will called one of his fellow partners in his practice, and he made calls to spread the word to others at work. Will works with truly wonderful men and women. His partners and the ladies in his office covered for him, taking great care of his patients, cancelling and rescheduling patients for clinic and surgery.

Before leaving for Jackson, Will wanted the six of us to sit down together so he could explain to the children what had happened. It was excruciating watching them get up, get ready, and eat their breakfast. It was so painful to watch them have their last few minutes of innocence before dropping this bomb on them. As we had already decided to keep them home from school and science fair projects were due that day, I silently slipped out of the house and placed their projects on the front porch. I texted my precious friend and carpool partner, Janet, with the news, and she offered to swing by to get their projects on the way to school.

We sat down with the kids in our den, and my dear husband, as gently as he could, explained to them what had happened to their grandmother the night before. Uncontrollable sobs overtook Will, me, and a couple of the kids, while the other two sat in silence with wide eyes, staring at us. For a while no one spoke, then came the questions. "Why would Pop do that to Grandmother?" "Is Pop in jail?" And, "What about our science projects?" "Are we going to school today?" Such difficult questions, with no real answers at this point.

We said goodbye to Will, and I texted and emailed all the people I could think of. I needed help. I needed people. Pretty soon, the phone calls and knocks on the door began. My precious friend of many years, Kristin Crook, arrived, tears in her eyes. Many of us feel the need to talk at a time like this, but she is one who has the ministry of presence. Kristin did not ask questions or press for details; she was just there with us. She sat with me for several hours that day, staying right by my side as people called and came and went from the house.

We had only been at Christ Presbyterian Church for a few months, but pastors David Filson and Todd Teller came, offering hugs, their presence, and words of comfort for the kids and me. I will never forget David saying as he walked in the door, "I am so sorry…I have no words." Soon, dear Shelly Sandoval arrived on our doorstep, with tears in her eyes as well.

My parents had plans to travel to North Carolina to spend a long weekend with Jeff and his family. Traveling with Mom was such a monumental effort, and they were already packed, so I encouraged them to keep their plans. On their way out of town, they came by to see us.

One of my new Bible study small group leaders, Kathy White, brought lunch and sat and ate with Kristin and me. And soon our other small group leader, Karen Anderson, called to say that she would be coming by later. I was amazed by the love and care shown by these dear friends, as I had only known them since January.

Soon, the living room of our home began to fill. Mary Lynn Giles, a precious friend and pastor's wife from our previous church, arrived. And Pam Benton, a dear family friend of thirty-five years. And then Karen Anderson.

I began to do laundry, since I knew the kids and I would probably be leaving for Jackson the next day. These dear women kept me company, helping to fold laundry. I was desperate for information from Will as he arrived in Jackson. There was just not much news. There was talk of Dad being transferred to a mental hospital for evaluation, but that did not happen.

There was so much confusion, and I felt the same need to time travel, to turn the clock back, as I had when my mom had her accident. My mind wanted to go back just twenty-four hours, so I kept thinking about yesterday at this same time. What seemed like such normalcy—laundry, kids going to school, grocery shopping—suddenly seemed a fading memory. Will's mom was alive yesterday at this time. If we could somehow just get back there. I pictured what Will's parents might have been doing this time yesterday. They might have spent time tending to their roses and then gone for a walk. She probably worked on a watercolor at her easel. Did she have any idea how their day would end?

As the afternoon wore on, my dear friends began to leave the house. Catha cooked dinner and brought it to us. Once she left, the kids and I were alone for the first time all day. I remember just staring into the oven, watching the food heat, when the phone rang. It was Angie Gage from church calling to check on us. I just sobbed and sobbed on the phone with her. I told her about God's timing with her phone call, about how he had sent people to be with us all day, and how her call came right after the last person had left.

I finally heard from Will that the funeral would be on Saturday, so I began to prepare to leave town in the morning. Sweet Emily did not have a spring dress for Grandmother's funeral, and I could not imagine going out to a public place and trying to act normal. So Shelly and her daughter Marisa came over that evening and took Emily to the mall to shop for some dresses and shoes.

In Jackson that morning, Dad had made his initial appearance in court. In spite of his medical conditions, he was denied bond and kept in jail.

*****

To outside observers and those taking in the news headlines, this seemed like a straightforward murder. But things are not always what they seem, and there is always a family and a story behind the murder headlines. I just never thought it would be ours.

Chapter 3

Boy Meets Girl

In the summer of 1995, I moved to Jackson, Mississippi, in all honesty in hopes of finding a husband. At the age of twenty-four, I was leaving the small town that I had mostly grown up in. It would be my first time ever living in a different town from my parents. I was afraid.

With two years of teaching elementary school under my belt, I landed a job teaching fifth-graders in a rural community outside of Jackson. In addition to teaching full-time, I was also able to pick up a coaching job. After school every day, I drove straight to the pool to coach the youngest swimmers of Sunkist Swim Team.

Soon I joined First Presbyterian Church of Jackson, and almost immediately I found myself embraced by the church's vibrant singles group. It was a beautiful community of young adults who loved to worship, serve, and do life together.

Within a few months, I met a very handsome medical school student who was a member of another church in town but attended our singles Bible study. One Monday night, I kept feeling a bump on the back of my chair during the study. I turned around several times to see him in the chair behind me, smiling back at me. Then, after a Sunday afternoon game of ultimate frisbee, we spent some time sitting and talking under a tree. He had also been asking my friend and roommate Laura Deadwyler about me, and in March of 1996, he took me on our first date.

Over a delicious dinner at Amerigo, we learned we had much in common, including our testimonies. They were not dramatic experiences, but Jesus had captured our hearts very early in life, and neither of us remembered a time we didn't know him. We had both grown up in Christian homes and had been very involved in Reformed University Fellowship at our respective universities. For both of us, it was through this ministry that our faith became our own. At RUF summer conference when I was twenty-one, the Lord used a sermon on grace to open my eyes to understand that my salvation was a free gift. It had nothing to do with anything I had ever done. This was a radical shift in my thinking and in my heart.

After dinner, we went to see the movie *Mr. Holland's Opus*, which was perfect, since we were both band geeks! As we talked through our band stories, we realized that we had both made Mississippi Lions' All-State Band our senior years of high school. He had graduated from high school a year after me. His Lions' Band group trained in Cleveland at Delta State University, and I had gone out most days to watch them march. I had been watching him and his group almost six years earlier!

Over the next week or so, we spent a good bit of time together, baking cookies, cooking dinners, and talking. A week and a half after our first date, he sat me down on the porch swing and told me he did not want to date me just to date but instead with the intent of seeing if we were compatible for marriage. I wholeheartedly agreed to this plan, and then he asked to hold my hand.

By the time summer came, we had met each other's parents and had spent lots of time together. Will had surgery to remove hardware surgically placed the year before to repair a badly broken collarbone, the result of a mountain biking accident. I went to visit him at his parents' house, where he was recovering. I knew he had enjoyed Legos as a child, so I brought along a little Lego set for him to do while he recovered. His mom later said that that was the moment she knew I was the one! A few days after his surgery, we ran a 5K, and it might have been a bit too much too soon, because his shirt had blood on it from the incision by the end of the race.

At some point that summer, we agreed that it might be time for our parents to meet one another. My parents came to Jackson to have dinner with Will's parents and Will and me. I have such sweet memories of that dinner at Olive Garden.

Bill and Susan Mayfield and Doug and Lynn Wheeler had so much in common with one another, and from the moment they met that night, the conversation flowed easily. Our parents hit it off so well that Will and I have often laughed that the two of us could have easily slipped out of the booth and left the restaurant, and the four of them would never have noticed!

*****

While our families of origin and our parents had much in common, there were also significant differences that shaped us.

Will's parents, Bill and Susan, had met on a blind date when they were in school at Millsaps College. Their courtship included many shared friends, weekends at their parents' houses, and even a choir tour to Mexico. They were married in June of 1968 in her hometown of Somerville, Tennessee.

After finishing at Millsaps, Bill began medical school at the University of Mississippi Medical Center, and Susan was a music teacher. Upon Bill's graduation from medical school, they moved to Birmingham for his residency in ophthalmology. It was during residency that Will was born. Bill had been drafted during Vietnam, and he served at the Naval Hospital in Jacksonville, Florida, for part of his residency.

When Will was four years old, the family moved back to Jackson, Mississippi, where Bill began his private practice. Will's younger brother Nick was born, and then when Will was ten years old, his youngest brother Alex was born.

The Mayfield household was busy and full of life with three boys around, and Susan greatly enjoyed getting to be a stay-at-home mother. She taught piano lessons in their home, including to her own boys. She faithfully taught the boys about the Christian faith, often quizzing them on the catechism as they jumped on the trampoline.

The family was very involved in their church, school, sports, band, and Boy Scouts. Susan and Bill encouraged the boys as they took up new musical instruments, and they spent many Friday nights at football games cheering on the marching band the boys were a part of. They also supported all three boys as they achieved the rank of Eagle Scout.

Susan was a beauty and had a striking resemblance to Jackie Kennedy, so much so that friends encouraged her to enter look-alike contests. But that was not of interest to her. Instead, she spent many hours serving their community, their church, and on the school board at Jackson Academy.

In addition to caring for his patients in his practice, Bill faithfully served their church, Covenant Presbyterian. He served as an elder, and he would later lead the church in the process of leaving their denomination and joining a new one.

Susan and Bill were master gardeners, and they spent many hours together tending gorgeous roses and other plants in their yard. They generously shared their roses with others, taking them to the sick, shut-ins, or those who just needed some encouragement. They also shared a mutual love of music, singing together in the church choir. Susan started and directed the church handbell choir, and Bill often played trumpet during services. He also enjoyed playing in the community band.

They both enjoyed exercising, and they took frequent walks together in their neighborhood. In the kitchen, they were a great team. Susan was an excellent cook, and Bill faithfully cleaned up and washed the dishes after every meal. Their marriage was their first priority as far as relationships went. They truly loved each other.

As Will grew older, he spent many summers at camp. He loved camp and was so happy there that he did not take the time to write home. Will said his mother got so accustomed to not receiving mail from him that it would have worried her to find a letter from him in the mail!

The Mayfields enjoyed family vacations, some of which included Susan's sisters, Helen, Amelia, and Frances, along with their families. They also spent time with their grandparents in Somerville,

Tennessee, and in Taylorsville, Mississippi, where Bill was raised. Will has many fond memories of their time spent in Taylorsville when he was growing up, playing in the rock quarry and riding go-carts.

In addition to his studies, Will was very focused on becoming an excellent trumpet player. He auditioned for Mississippi Lions' All-State Band all four years of high school. His senior year, he finally made it. Lions' Band was a family affair for the Mayfields. Will's Dad had played trumpet in Lions' Band when he was in high school, and Will's brother Nick would eventually make the band as well, joining their percussion section.

Upon graduation from Jackson Academy, Will went to study at Vanderbilt University, earning a degree in molecular biology. At Vanderbilt, he was very involved in Reformed University Fellowship and had wonderful friends in the ministry.

Knowing that he wanted to be a physician, Will studied for and took the MCAT and applied for admission to medical school. In 1994, he moved back to Jackson to begin medical school at the University of Mississippi Medical Center, where his dad had gone to school and where his brother Nick would also later go to medical school.

My parents, Doug and Lynn, were also college sweethearts. They were both music majors at West Chester State, in Pennsylvania, and they married in June of 1968 after Doug graduated. They both took jobs as music teachers in the area, but when I was born, they decided that Mom would stay home with me.

Lynn had grown up in Philadelphia and a nearby suburb, and Doug was raised in West Chester, so our little family enjoyed frequent visits with my nearby grandparents, aunts, uncles, and cousins.

A year after my sister Susan was born, we packed up and left the Philadelphia area, as well as all of our extended family. We headed west, way west, to Colorado Springs, where Dad joined the percussion section of the Air Force Academy band. My brother Jeff was born the following year.

My parents made the decision for Mom to stay home with us in those early years. Money was tight, but we had what we needed. There were no family vacations. Instead, there were family outings, taking full advantage of our beautiful location. We often drove the Pikes Peak Highway to the 14,115-foot summit of Pikes Peak. We spent time on the Air Force Academy campus, going to concerts and other events. We went camping in our Volkswagen van, which had a mini refrigerator, a Porta Potti, a foldout bed, and a pop-up tent. I remember settling in at bedtime in the pop-up tent with my siblings, listening to the night sounds in the woods, the cool mountain air entering the unzipped flaps of the tent. We visited Garden of the Gods, Cave of the Winds, and many other wonderful places.

After serving in the Air Force Academy band for four years, Dad took a position as a music professor at Delta State University in Cleveland, Mississippi. That's right. Cleveland is in the heart of the Mississippi Delta, the flattest land you can imagine—mile after mile of farmland growing cotton, soybeans, and rice; elevation 141 feet. No view of Pikes Peak from the kitchen window. The first time we drove from Colorado to Mississippi, Mom sobbed as we drove over the last hill and into the Delta.

In spite of the difficult geographical changes, our family soon settled in and felt at home in this tiny Southern town. Dad settled into teaching percussion at the university, and Mom soon took a job teaching elementary music at Presbyterian Day School. She also taught private piano and guitar lessons, and she eventually started an excellent boys' choir at the school.

We also joined First Presbyterian Church, and later, Covenant Presbyterian Church. Mom and Dad sang in the choir. Dad eventually served the church as a deacon and then as an elder, and my siblings and I were involved in all the children's programs.

With Mom and Dad both working as teachers, finances were very tight. Dad sometimes picked up extra jobs to help make ends meet, including a summer working at a catfish farm in town. Mom eventually started coaching the local swim team, going straight to the pool after teaching music all day.

Shortly after moving to Mississippi, Dad decided to pursue a doctorate degree from the University of Northern Colorado in Greeley. So for four years in a row, we moved back out to Colorado to spend our summers there.

Those were good summers. When Dad was in class and study-ing during the week, Mom took us swimming and signed us all up for the library's summer reading program. Rocky Mountain National Park was not far from Greeley, so we spent many of our Saturdays hiking in the park and enjoying Estes Park as a family. Of course, we were exposed to plenty of music, attending many concerts at the university. Mom and Dad purchased my first flute for me, a hun-dred-dollar used instrument, and Dad began to teach me to play.

Before the last summer of graduate school, Dad took a semester sabbatical from his job at DSU. He went to Colorado alone for the winter and spring terms to get more coursework done toward his degree. It was not an easy time; we missed him, and Mom juggled full-time work and taking care of three kids without him. Dad had very little money to live on, but he often sent money and birthday presents for us, even if it meant he would have to do without. We joined him in Colorado for that last summer as he finished school, and then we celebrated the culmination of his hard work at his graduation.

When I was in middle school, we moved away for two more summers. Mom and Dad took summer jobs at a YMCA camp on Cape Cod. My siblings and I were campers for the summers. Sometimes we lived in the cabins with other campers our ages, and other weeks we chose to live in the little cottage with our parents.

Since Mississippi was so far from our extended family, we spent many school breaks and holidays traveling to Pennsylvania and Cape Cod to spend time with grandparents, aunts, uncles, and cousins.

Mom and Dad taught us what it meant to serve others. We spent many Sunday afternoons visiting shut-ins as a family, in spite of the many protests from my siblings and me. I learned many important lessons from those dear folks, and I am thankful our parents made us go and participate. My parents were hospitable, frequently inviting others into our home for meals.

My high school years were filled with hours of marching band, lifeguarding, and studying. Upon graduating, I attended Delta State, as I was not yet ready to leave home. When I was not studying, at band rehearsals, or at swim practice, I coached the local swim team with Mom.

After graduating with a degree in elementary education, I took a teaching job at a school there in Cleveland. I also continued to coach with Mom after school. In addition to becoming running partners, we developed an even deeper mother-daughter friendship.

Having such a close relationship with Mom made it difficult to consider moving away, but I knew it was time.

Chapter 4

A Beautiful, Imperfect Beginning

In the fall of 1996, six months into our dating relationship, Will and I went camping with some friends outside of Mentone, Alabama, near Alpine Camp, where he had spent a summer as a counselor. We went down to Little River Canyon, and one by one, the guys helped all the ladies climb down into the canyon by the only way down. We had to descend by climbing down two trees, and I was terrified! Will had been so excited to share this with me as he had done this with his campers several years earlier.

One night, he took me on a hike to watch the sunset, and he asked me if he was the kind of guy I would marry. Of course, my answer was yes! Not long after this, as he hugged me good night after a date, he said, "I'm sure you're wondering why I haven't kissed you yet." He went on to explain that while he really wanted to, he was convicted about the importance of being careful physically in our relationship.

On November 16, Will picked me up for a "surprise" date. He handed me the first of ten envelopes containing original poetry giving me clues about where to go to find the next clue. We had a lot of laughs along the way that night as we drove all over Jackson finding clues. Along the way, we had a lovely dinner, and the final clue took us to his parents' lake house. His friend Todd Kistemaker had set the stage before we arrived. As we walked into the house, there was soft classical piano music playing on the CD player. Candles were lit, rose petals were scattered on the coffee table, and there was an ice bucket with champagne. We talked for a bit, and then he handed me a children's board book called *Hush, Little Baby*, and he had me read it aloud until I got to the page that said, "Daddy's gonna buy you a diamond ring." There, in a cut-out in the book, was a beautiful diamond engagement ring! He asked me if I would be his wife, and I answered yes as he slipped the ring onto my finger. Then he asked if he could kiss me. What a gift he gave me, or rather us, by waiting until our engagement night to kiss me for the very first time. It was worth the wait!

Of course, our parents already knew that he was going to ask me to marry him, but it was so fun to call them and tell them our news. The next morning, I had to drive to Hattiesburg to coach a swim meet, and it was fun to get to tell the story to team parents and coaches.

The engagement ring Will gave me was one that he had saved for and had chosen and purchased himself, and it was lovely. He gave me a choice, though, between the one he had purchased and one that he had inherited from his grandmother. Since Will was her oldest grandson, his paternal grandmother left this ring to him in her will. Before even seeing it, I told him I would love to have the family ring. It symbolizes legacies of faithful marriages, as it holds both his great-grandmother's and his grandmother's engagement diamonds. In the center sits the diamond Will's grandfather Cato gave to his wife, Jane, for their fortieth anniversary.

We set a wedding date of June 28, once his third year of medical school was over and I was done teaching for the summer.

Our engagement was a sweet time, filled with fun family time and showers and parties given by family and friends. We got together with our parents often, running 5K's in Jackson and competing in mini triathlons together in Cleveland with dear family friends, including Bill and Susan Wolters.

Will's mother was thrilled about having a daughter in the family, and she often took me shopping for clothes. Even though I did not have plans to choose a silver pattern, she insisted that I do so. To be sure that I took care of it, she picked me up and took me to the silver store herself!

It was also a very intentional time, as Will led us well in preparing for our marriage, not just the wedding. He sought counsel from friends who had recently gotten married and from campus ministers and pastors. He purchased two copies of several recommended books on marriage, and we read them and discussed them. We also did some premarital counseling with my pastor, Tim Starnes, who would officiate for us.

*****

The evening before our wedding, we had a joy-filled time with family and friends at our lovely rehearsal dinner, hosted by Will's parents. And of course, there was music. Will's mother and her sisters, Amelia and Frances, wrote some hilarious original lyrics to familiar tunes for us. They sang, and our dads played duets; my dad on harmonica and Will's dad on accordion. There were also heartfelt toasts, and it all made for a beautiful evening of laughter, tears, and smiles. June 27 also happened to be Will's dad's birthday. He pulled me aside later that evening, and with a twinkle in his eye, said that it was the nicest birthday party he had ever thrown for himself.

June 28 came, and my parents provided a lovely church wedding and reception. We were surrounded by family and friends. My grandmothers were elderly and unable to travel the many miles from Pennsylvania to be there with us. Our precious family friend Liba Dean, who had suffered the horrific effects of severe rheumatoid arthritis, was wheeled up to the place where my grandmothers would have sat.

Given our mutual love of music, we had the glorious sounds of trumpets, a flute, an organ, and a vocal soloist. We also had a congregational hymn after Dad walked me down the aisle.

When we were planning the service, we chose "The Church's One Foundation" (Samuel S. Wesley, 1864). The wedding planner asked which verses we would like to sing. Even though we both knew the hymn well, we had not really thought about how many verses there were. Since we were both lovers of hymns, we said that of course we wanted all the verses. After about the third verse, our wedding party began to smile and snicker around us. Yes, we finished the hymn, singing all six verses! To this day, any time we sing that wonderful hymn, Will and I catch one another's eyes and smile.

We were as clueless as most young couples on their wedding days as we gazed into one another's eyes, repeating our wedding vows. We had no idea what words such as "for better or for worse" really meant, and that is probably a blessing.

From watching my interactions with my parents throughout our engagement, Will could tell that "leaving and cleaving" was going to be a struggle for me. He was right. Mom and I were very close friends, and he knew a shift needed to happen in order for us to have a successful marriage. Will needed to become my best friend. Before leaving for our honeymoon, he talked to me about how he thought it would be a good idea for us not to call our parents while on our honeymoon. I thought it seemed a little extreme, but later I realized just how important it was in helping us to bond as a couple. In the almost two weeks that we were on our honeymoon, not talking to my mom was so important in helping me to begin to understand what it really meant to leave my parents and cleave to my new husband.

We were soon off to Memphis to spend our wedding night at the Peabody Hotel. The next day, we began the two-day drive to Estes Park, Colorado, for our honeymoon. We stayed in a little cabin and enjoyed a week of hiking and sightseeing together. Our evenings were spent on our little front porch, stargazing and discussing our dreams and future. Today, hiking in the mountains continues to be our favorite activity, but as newlyweds we never could have imagined the conversations we would have or the tears we would shed as we hiked together years in the future.

*****

The summer of 1997 was one of settling into married life and making a home of our little six-hundred-square-foot apartment on the campus of the University of Mississippi Medical Center. Being in the same town as Will's parents, we enjoyed frequent dinners and time with them. I called them Mom and Dad, and Will did the same with my parents. We were both grateful for these close relationships with our parents and in-laws.

Later that summer, I remembered that I had not closed the individual checking account I had before we were married. I knew it was empty, but I made a trip to the bank to sign papers to close it. The teller asked how I would like to take out what was in the account. I told her there was nothing left in it. She said, "No, you have six hundred dollars left in the account." I could not believe it! I still have no idea where that money came from. Not long after this, we received a bill for sinus surgery I had had the month before our wedding. The amount we owed almost exactly equaled the mysterious amount that was in my checking account. We were so grateful for God's provision in this!

Will began his last year of medical school, juggling studies, rotations in several specialties, and traveling around to interview for residency programs. I began another year of teaching first grade and continuing to coach the swim team. My income barely supported us, but we had what we needed.

At First Presbyterian, we joined a Sunday school class for young married couples, and we continued to grow under the preaching of our pastor, Ligon Duncan. His wife, Anne, took it upon herself to mentor a group of young wives, leading us through a Bible study in their home. The wisdom she taught and shared with us was very impactful on me as a new young wife.

We sang in the church choir together, singing beautiful works by Brahms, Rutter, and so many others. I also had the opportunity to play flute in church occasionally. It was fun to get to share our love of music.

In the evenings, we shared joys and frustrations of our work. My work was a mix of excitement over seeing my students progress with their reading and other skills, frustration with behavioral problems, and the sadness over some of my children coming to school hungry because they had not had breakfast that morning. In the meantime,

Will was having a difficult time narrowing down specialties because he was enjoying so much of what he was doing.

His month spent in labor and delivery was a sweet time. I can still remember the look on his face in the evenings as he told me about delivering babies that day. He was in awe of life and the Creator. He really enjoyed ophthalmology and the intricacies of the eye. The hand had also been fascinating to him in gross anatomy. And (back to the Legos) he enjoyed putting things together and repairing them, and in the end, he chose orthopaedic surgery.

Spring came, and with it came the "Match," the event when medical school students find out where they will do their residency training. It is a stressful event. The entire graduating class and their families would be in a room together. Each person's name and where they will go for residency is read aloud in front of the entire group. You find out where you are going in front of everyone!

Will had ranked quite a few programs, and orthopaedics was particularly competitive at the time. His name was read aloud, and it was announced that he would be training at the University of South Alabama in Mobile. While it was not one of his top choices, we were thankful for him to have a spot.

May brought Will's graduation, the end of my school year, house hunting, and the beginnings of the transition from Jackson to Mobile. We bought a cute little eighty-year-old, thousand-square-foot house near downtown. We spent the summer getting settled and welcoming our new puppy, Allie, an English springer spaniel Will had given me for my birthday. To earn some extra money, I worked a miserable job answering phones at a temp agency.

In mid-July, I went home to Cleveland to celebrate my brother's wedding to Wendy, his high-school sweetheart. Because Will had just started his intern year a couple of weeks earlier, he was not able to be there for the wedding. Asking for time off just days after beginning his residency would have been a foolish idea, but I was still pretty upset with him for not coming with me to the wedding. This was really my first taste of what life married to a surgeon was going to look like, and I had a lot to learn about just how different schedules and family life can look with a physician in the family.

In August, I began teaching seventh-grade math and remedial reading at an inner-city middle school in Mobile. It was not the easiest transition; my job was difficult and very frustrating at times, and we were away from our parents. Will worked long hours and had in-house call, which sometimes had him staying at the hospital from Friday morning until Monday night. To get some time together on those weekends, I occasionally took dinner to the hospital, where we would eat and visit in the doctor's lounge.

We rode out our very first hurricane in October, Hurricane Georges. Will was at the hospital when it hit, so he had to stay at the hospital for the next twenty-four hours. It was a scary night by myself with no power, so I invited my sweet elderly neighbor and her son over to cook dinner on our gas stove. We had a fun time visiting over a candlelit dinner, and I was so thankful for the company.

In January, we learned we were expecting our first baby. We were thrilled! Even though it would be a sacrifice financially, the plan was for me to finish the school year in June and not go back to teaching in the fall.

Chapter 5

The Thrill of New Life and Growing Pains

On September 23, 1999, we received the beautiful gift of Emily Claire Mayfield. All four grandparents made it to the hospital just before the delivery, and they were able to meet her moments after she was born. We have a precious photo of all four of our parents surrounding the hospital bed that Will and I are sitting on with newborn Emily. I thought it was the picture of perfection. Life could not get any better. Heaven on earth. At that moment, I could never have imagined the tragedies that would unfold and take three of our parents out of the picture by the time that sweet baby girl was sixteen.

We began settling into life as a family of three. We were pretty typical new parents, navigating newborn feeding and sleeping schedules, reading parenting books to be sure we were on track, and trying to make time for our marriage. I loved my new role as a mother and cherished the time I had with Emily. We spent holidays and many weekends with our extended family.

In December, we celebrated the wedding of Nick, Will's brother. It was a joyous occasion welcoming our dear new sister-in-law, Tanya, into the family. She was a gorgeous bride, and the church was decorated so beautifully for Christmas. We had a wonderful weekend spending time with extended family, many of whom got to meet baby Emily for the first time.

Back home in Mobile, we spent our days on playgroup outings with a group of residents' wives and their babies. We also spent time with my sister Susan, who was working as an EMT in town. In the fall of 2000, Susan married Todd, so we had another in-law. Our family was growing! We were also involved in a great church, but it was across the bay, so I was rather lonely at times. This and other reasons led us to find a church closer to home.

Will continued to progress through residency, and in the summer of 2001, we moved into a little apartment in New Orleans so that Will could complete a three-month rotation at Children's Hospital. It was a hot summer, and I was pregnant with baby number two, so I was grateful for the many pools and streams throughout the apartment complex. Will worked very long and late hours, so Emily and I spent our days exploring the pools around our summer home. We were also blessed with fun visits from grandparents: visiting the zoo, aquarium, and other nearby attractions. Worshiping at Redeemer Presbyterian on Sundays was a sweet time. Emily was well-loved in Sunday school, and we enjoyed the distinct flavor of New Orleans jazz in the worship service, as well as the faithful preaching.

It was a good summer, but we were so happy to move back home to Mobile at the end of September. Being in the port city of New Orleans during 9/11 had been somewhat unnerving, and I was thankful to be home and closer to my doctor since I was now seven months pregnant.

That fall, Will's family came to Mobile to celebrate Thanksgiving with us. They helped us put up our Christmas tree a little early, and a few days later, on November 27, William Cato Mayfield IV arrived in the world. As when Emily was born, we were blessed with great help from our parents. My mom spent a week helping us get adjusted, followed by a week with Will's mom.

During my mom's stay with us, she could tell that something was not quite right with me. After delivering Emily, I was very weepy and would cry every afternoon for a few weeks, which was not terribly unusual postpartum behavior. But this time was different. I was very down and struggling to bond with the baby. When William was a few weeks old, Mom came back and offered to take Emily home with her for a week or so. I felt guilty letting my two-year-old go away, but that time was so beneficial and brought much healing. It was a special time bonding and snuggling with my precious new baby boy, and Emily had a great time with my parents!

In fact, it was around this time that Emily gave my mom, who up until this point had been "Grandmom," a new name that stuck. Mom and Emily shared a graham cracker, each biting opposite ends. They laughed, and Emily called her graham. Mom thought she would love to be called "Gram," so that was what the grandchildren called her from then on.

That winter, the residency program decided at the last minute to add another away rotation. So in January, with a two-year-old and a newborn in tow, we packed up and headed to Birmingham for Will to complete a two-month foot-and-ankle rotation.

Will's parents helped us move into the tiny efficiency apartment in Birmingham. I was undone at being uprooted after having just had a baby, and I was probably still dealing with some postpartum depression. As Mom and Dad were about to leave, I remember sitting on the edge of the bed and sobbing. I had never been one to cry in front of others if I could hold it in, but I was a mess.

The apartment was less than ideal for a family of four, all four of us sleeping, cooking, and eating in one room. Newborn William slept at the foot of our bed in the playpen, and Emily slept on a pallet on the floor under the kitchen table draped with a blanket to keep out the light. We were in downtown Birmingham, it was bitter cold, and there was nowhere inside for Emily to run around and play. We had no extra money to spend on fun indoor outings in the city.

Three weeks into our time there, my nerves were shot. Will and I decided it might be best for me and the kids to find a better place to stay while he finished the rotation. So we packed up and left. We spent half the time with Will's parents and half the time with mine. It was a sweet time with the kids' grandparents, and I was so grateful for the extra help with Emily and William, but I missed Will terribly. Once his time in Birmingham ended, we were happy to be reunited together again at home in Mobile.

Settled in at home, it was a joy watching our kids grow and interact with each other. Emily loved baby William and being a big sister, and William loved her. They shared a bedroom in our tiny house, and some of the sweetest times were listening to them interact after we tucked them into bed at night. Emily would tell William the stories from the books she had in her bed, and he would babble and laugh.

We continued to enjoy sweet time with our parents, as they came to visit us in Mobile as often as they were able. Oh, how our toddlers loved this time with their grandparents! Saturday morning strolls to the Krispy Kreme around the corner from our house became a tradition when my parents visited. Every time Will's parents visited, they brought roses from their yard. Emily and Grandmother often spent time together arranging the gorgeous flowers in vases.

Will's parents, being master gardeners, loved walks through our neighborhood to admire the flowers that grew in this tropical climate. We tagged along with the stroller and our springer spaniel, Allie. On one occasion, Will's mother reached down to cup and admire what she called a rare flower. Before we realized what was happening, Allie lunged toward the flower and ate it out of her hand. Mom Mayfield gasped in disbelief! The rest of us laughed and laughed at her shock.

The last year of Will's training was a busy one. We traveled a good bit to interview with orthopaedic groups all over the southeast. Will also interviewed and applied for several sports fellowship programs. When those fell through, we focused on praying about where God would have him settle down to practice medicine.

But in the spring, Will heard about a fellowship spot that had unexpectedly come open, and he really wanted to apply. I was not exactly thrilled about the thought of another year of training. The years in training had been very lean financially, and I was afraid we might not be able to make ends meet. There had been times in the past few years when the money was gone for the month. We were out of milk, and payday was still days away. I would dig through the children's piggy banks for money to buy a half gallon of milk. I had seen God provide time after time, but I was still afraid.

Will was so excited about the possibility of this opportunity, and it was a rare occurrence for a spot to come available. So I agreed that he should pursue it. He applied, and he was offered the spot at Cincinnati SportsMedicine and Orthopaedic Center. This is a highly sought-after fellowship program, and it was truly amazing the way God orchestrated this to happen for Will.

*****

In the summer of 2003, my dad took a position as the chair of the music department at Clayton State University. So after twenty-five years in Cleveland, my parents moved to the Atlanta area. They joined Covenant Presbyterian Church in Fayetteville, where Mom began to serve as the director of children's ministry.

Later that summer, with the help of Will's parents and mine, we moved our little family to Cincinnati, Ohio, for one year. Emily and William made fun memories with all four grandparents while Will and I worked on unpacking and settling into our cozy little nine-hundred-square-foot apartment.

The kids and their grandparents played around the apartment complex, feeding the geese and enjoying the pool. They also explored the fabulous Cincinnati Zoo and came home giggling. The grandparents said, "Now please don't tell your parents what we fed you for lunch." Of course, Emily and William both immediately yelled, "Ice cream! We had ice cream for lunch!"

I was not planning to get too invested in our new city, since we would only be there for such a short time. But, as usual, God had different plans. We immediately found a wonderful church home at North Cincinnati Community Church, where a sweet small group took us in, and I attended a women's Bible study. We also found a wonderful preschool for Emily across the street from our apartment. It was a short but sweet year enjoying new friends and exploring the city. Will's fellowship was a great fit for him, and he was studying with and working under several excellent surgeons.

Once again, the job search was underway. Will's parents were still in Jackson, Mississippi, and my parents were now in the Atlanta area, so we traveled around looking at practices in the southeast that would be within driving distance of our parents. A great group in the Nashville area offered him a job. Will had loved living in Nashville during his years at Vanderbilt, and we felt like it would be a great place to raise a family.

That summer, we celebrated our last wedding of a sibling when Will's brother Alex married Jenny. It was a joy to welcome another dear sister-in-law and her precious little boy Peyton into the Mayfield family.

At the end of one year of fellowship training, we left the great city of Cincinnati richer in friendship and faith. Will was well-prepared to begin his practice. Oh, and we left with a four-year-old, a two-year-old, and baby number three on the way.

Chapter 6

Settling Down and Becoming Unsettled

We moved to the Nashville area in August of 2004, got settled into our new home, and found a new church home. Will started work. This was what Will had been preparing for over the past ten years. After four years of medical school, five years of residency, and a one-year fellowship, he was finally beginning his practice! It was exciting and also a bit daunting.

On our first Sunday at church, we ran into Bill and Christie Hart. Christie had been involved in RUF at Vanderbilt with Will, and she grabbed me, said we would be friends, and invited me to a playgroup at Wendy Twit's house. We had not found a preschool for Emily and William for the school year, so I needed a playgroup. Those were sweet Fridays with Christie, Wendy, and the rest of the group.

On October 26, Luke Douglas Mayfield was born, making us a family of five. Will and I were so grateful to have been given these three healthy children, and we all quickly grew to love this precious new baby boy.

In November, at the age of ninety, my maternal grandmother went home to be with Jesus. So when Luke was just a few weeks old, the kids and I, along with Mom and Dad, flew to Philadelphia for her funeral.

Not long after the death of her mother, my mom began experiencing some health problems. We were all concerned. I have a very vivid memory of us on the way to church one Sunday during that time. We were talking about what was going on with Mom, and I looked at Will and said, "If something happens to her, I don't know what I would do without my mom." Other than Will, she was my best friend.

By January, it was discovered that Mom had a large ovarian cyst, and her doctor was convinced that it was benign. In February of 2005, on her fifty-eighth birthday, she had surgery to have it removed. Dad called us crying after the surgery and said they found some cancer inside the cyst. He put the surgeon on the phone with Will to explain. Soon, we learned that the diagnosis was stage 2 ovarian cancer, and that she would need to undergo both radiation and chemotherapy.

We went to visit Mom and Dad fairly often as she recovered from surgery and went through treatment from March into the fall. Dad took wonderful care of Mom; it was sweet to watch. He lovingly took care of her chemotherapy port site, and he took on extra chores around the house.

Mom had been the most active person I had ever known. She was an elementary music teacher, a swim coach, a runner, a children's ministry director at church, and an amazing wife, mother, and grandmother. Now she was learning to pace herself and to take days to sit and rest and recover from treatments. She spent hours reading the Bible and praying, and she was an encouragement to us all. She adopted the hymn, "Whate'er My God Ordains Is Right" as her theme song, and we would often sing it when our family was together, led by Will on the guitar.

> Whate'er my God ordains is right: his holy will
> abideth;
> I will be still whate'er he doth, and follow where
> he guideth.
> He is my God; though dark my road,
> He holds me that I shall not fall: wherefore to
> him I leave it all.

Whate'er my God ordains is right: he never will
    deceive me;
He leads me by the proper path; I know he will
    not leave me.
I take, content, what he hath sent;
His hand can turn my griefs away, and patiently
    I wait his day.
Whate'er my God ordains is right:
Though now this cup, in drinking,
May bitter seem to my faint heart, I take it, all
    unshrinking.
My God is true; each morn anew
Sweet comfort yet shall fill my heart,
And pain and sorrow shall depart.
Whate'er my God ordains is right: here shall my
    stand be taken;
Though sorrow, need, or death be mine, yet I am
    not forsaken.
My Father's care is round me there;
He holds me that I shall not fall: and so to him I
    leave it all.

(Samuel Rodigast, 1675)

Emily started kindergarten that fall, William was in preschool, and we were enjoying all the first-year milestones with baby Luke. Mom and Dad came to visit us in September to celebrate Emily's birthday, and then again in October to celebrate Luke's first birthday. Mom was doing great. She had finished cancer treatments, her hair was beginning to grow back, and her post-treatment scan was clear! I breathed a sigh of relief that she had suffered, it was over, and we could now enjoy being a healthy, active family again with no more bumps in the road.

In November, they came back again to celebrate William's fourth birthday, and Mom took him on a sweet little date to Panera to get his favorite bagels and to read his favorite books together. On this visit, Mom and Dad were also able to attend Emily's kindergarten Thanksgiving program. Then our little family traveled to Jackson to spend Thanksgiving with the Mayfield side of the family, which now included two new cousins. Nick and Tanya welcomed precious Hannah Grace, and Alex and Jenny welcomed baby Drake earlier that year. Oh, how we just loved this family time!

Chapter 7

Where Are You, God?

January 2006

Following the traumatic Christmas Day accident that left her paralyzed, Mom remained in the intensive care unit in Atlanta Medical Center. She was in a Stryker bed that rotated from side to side in order to keep her from developing pressure sores. She was also under heavy sedation, as this type of bed created a huge amount of anxiety for the patient. Mom needed neck-stabilization surgery, but it had been postponed due to fluid in her lungs, as well as issues from her abdominal surgery.

At home in Nashville, we were doing what we could to maintain some sort of normalcy. Will was working, Emily was in kindergarten, and William was in preschool. I found the most mundane daily chores to be exhausting, and interacting with people on a daily basis was so hard. The most common conversational question asked in early January is, "How was your Christmas?" I did not feel ready to face that question yet. So I did all I could to avoid interactions with people, from friends who did not yet know what had happened, to the cashier in the grocery store. I struggled to look people in the eye because I either wanted to fall apart and tell the whole story or just not engage at all. It was hard to sleep, and I woke every morning with the immediate thought that it had all just been a nightmare, only to come to the cruel realization that it was true.

I felt myself often groping around in the dark for some hope. I did not want to hear verses that people would share or send, but I had this truth that God had given me: "I know God is sovereign, and I know he loves my parents." That was it, and I had to repeat it often to myself.

Around this time, God brought to mind a passage of Scripture I had memorized years earlier with my sweet friend and running partner Mindy Roberts. It became a lifeline for me, bringing a glimmer of hope during some of the darkest days, and I sent it to Dad. Second Corinthians 4:16–18 says,

> Therefore we do not lose heart. Though outwardly we are wasting away, yet inwardly we are being renewed day by day. For our light and momentary troubles are achieving for us an eternal glory that far outweighs them all. So we fix our eyes not on what is seen, but on what is unseen. For what is seen is temporary, but what is unseen is eternal. (NIV)

The people in our church in Nashville loved us well, checking on us and bringing meals. But because we were still fairly new to the Nashville area and because of the trauma we were walking through, we began to feel very overwhelmed being in a large church. At this point, we felt as though we needed to be in a smaller church that would feel more like a family. We began to visit a small church in our denomination, and they quickly drew us in and loved us.

One morning a few weeks after the accident, I buckled my three little ones into the van. As I got into the driver's seat, I turned to see little four-year-old William looking at all the seats around him. He looked at me and said, "Mommy, if we had just one more seat in our van, Gram could have ridden with us instead of having to ride in Uncle Jeff's car." I realized he had been counting the seats in the car. My heart had already been grieving for what my children were going through, but this interaction made me realize that they were also thinking through the what-ifs.

Back home in St. Louis, in addition to all the emotions from having been in the car with Mom, Jeff's family was still recovering from physical injuries sustained in the wreck. Jeff and Wendy were dealing with soreness and joint and back pain. Nelson had an additional X-ray, which revealed that his leg was indeed broken. And at their home in Georgia, Susan and Todd were wrestling with the major decision of how to help with Mom's care.

By mid-January, Mom was well enough for surgery, and on January 16, her neurosurgeon performed neck-stabilization surgery, fusing together her C1 and C2 vertebrae. The surgery went well, but several days later, she developed a staph infection. Because her neck was now stabilized, she was able to be in a TriaDyne bed, which adjusted airflow to keep her from developing pressure sores. This was much better than having to be in the rotating Stryker bed.

Dad went back to work, teaching percussion and overseeing the music department at Clayton State during the day. After work each night, he drove to the hospital to spend time with Mom. Then he would make the long drive home, try to sleep, and wake up the next morning to do it all again. He was exhausted, and he often told people, "It is well with my soul, but everything else is falling apart."

I was able to get back to Atlanta to see Mom, thanks to Will's mother coming to Nashville to help him take care of Emily and William while he worked. This gave them some fun time with Grandmother and a sense of normalcy. I took Luke with me, as I figured playing with a baby would be a good distraction for Dad.

It was such a hard visit. Mom had been under sedation, but they were decreasing the medications so that she could gradually come out of it. I could hardly stand to be in the room with her. Her eyes were open wider than I had ever seen them, a look of horror on her face. She was trying to mouth something, and terrible muffled cries were coming out of her. There was nothing we could do to help her. All I could do was stroke her cheek and tell her I loved her. This was the loneliest suffering I had ever witnessed. A kind of torture I could never have imagined.

As I watched her, I imagined Jesus on the cross, completely alone in his suffering, and the pain of the Father as he turned his back on his Son. I knew that unlike Jesus, Mom wasn't alone in her suffering. But even though my mind knew this to be true, I remember crying out to him, "Where are you?" I was angry with God and could not feel his presence. More than once, I made this demand of him: "You either have to heal her or take her home to heaven! You cannot leave her here like this!" I remember walking the halls with Dad, and all I could do was sob.

*****

Because Dad wanted to get Mom home, the goal was to secure a bed for her at Shepherd Center, which is a rehabilitation hospital for people with spinal cord and other catastrophic injuries. After spending six weeks in the ICU at Atlanta Medical Center, Mom was moved to Shepherd on February 10, in hopes of her rehabilitating enough to move home. She would need to learn to swallow, eat, talk, and drive her wheelchair with a mechanism in her mouth.

We were able to get to Atlanta to see her once she had been at Shepherd for a couple of weeks. Our whole family walked into the room to find her sitting up in her wheelchair. It was an emotional reunion, as it was the first time for the five of us to see her up in the chair, and it was the kids' first time to see her since the accident. While we were thankful to all be together, it was very difficult to see my spunky momma like this, strapped into a chair and unable to do anything for herself. Her hair had grown a good bit since the accident and was in very tight gray curls all over her head, leaving my young, once very active and healthy mom looking twenty years older. But as she smiled at us, I could see that the same spirit was still inside her. The boys seemed comfortable hugging her and touching her, but Emily was very apprehensive about getting close.

While we were in town, I was able to spend some time alone with her. There was a pen with a notebook next to her bed so that visitors could write down things she mouthed. She had a strong desire to communicate, but it was very tedious work. She painstakingly mouthed letters and words in an attempt to communicate thoughts and sentences. Mom had always loved people and communicating with them, and she was a Yankee, so she had always talked fast! As such, it was quite a challenge for her to slow down.

During her cancer treatment, Mom had committed Psalm 139 to memory. Upon truly waking from sedation after the accident and having an awareness of her condition, verse 16 was one of her first lucid thoughts, and she shared it, quoting it to Dad and others.

> Your eyes saw my unformed body; all the days ordained for me were written in your book before one of them came to be. (Psalm 139:16 NIV)

Now that she was fully awake and knew the details of the accident and what had happened at the scene, Mom began to call Will her hero. When introducing him to people, she often told them that he was her hero. He was not really thrilled with the attention Mom gave him for saving her life at the scene. He just did what he was trained to do in an event like this. Later, when talking about Will giving her mouth-to-mouth breathing, Mom began to joke with him saying, "Not many sons-in-law would do that to their mothers-in-law!"

Because Mom would require care around the clock once home, Susan and Todd made the decision to move in with Mom and Dad. They had been living less than two hours from Atlanta, and Todd's job already involved some travel in that part of Georgia. Susan would leave her job and become Mom's primary caregiver during the day. At the time of this decision, none of us had any idea just how all-consuming and difficult Mom's care would actually be, and I will forever be grateful to my sister for all that she sacrificed.

Mom and Dad's house was not handicap-accessible, so next came the daunting process of making modifications to the house. Shepherd Center had told Dad that she would be ready to be discharged around the middle of March. The deacons of their church built patios and ramps in the front and back of the house. Existing flooring was replaced with flooring that would allow the wheelchair to navigate more easily around the house. Contractors donated their time to widen doors. These friends and strangers were quite literally the hands and feet of Jesus. Without their willingness and skill, Mom would never have been able to enter her house again. In early March, Susan and Todd moved into the house.

Dad, Susan, Todd, and Marsha McKibben, who was a long-time family friend and also a registered nurse, went through intensive training at Shepherd, basically learning how to keep Mom alive in their care at home. They learned how to operate her ventilator and the cough machine, how to feed her, and what seemed like an endless list of other care issues.

Mom was also working hard, doing her part to rehabilitate enough to go home. She had to do swallow studies in order to be allowed to start eating pureed foods. For almost two months, her nutrition had come solely through liquids pushed through her feeding tube.

Learning how to talk was extremely difficult and demanding. For healthy people, the normal way of talking is to speak on the exhale. For someone on a ventilator, speaking is done on the inhale. Also the cuff on her trach had to be adjusted so that she could produce sound. It was a whole new way of speaking, but she worked hard to be able to communicate.

When a crisis comes, we often realize just how meaningful the little things in life are. Before the accident, Mom and I talked on the phone almost every day, and I loved our talks. After her injury, the absence of our frequent visits was painful. Mom could not pick up the phone and call, and I couldn't call her directly anymore.

I will never forget the first time a caregiver helped her call me. I answered the phone, and heard in a very labored effort, "Hi… Julie…it's…Mom." I silently cried into the phone as I realized just how much our relationship would change. Over the phone, someone would always be there listening to our conversation. Things would never be the same.

Mom also learned how to drive her power wheelchair through a device in her mouth called a "sip-and-puff straw." As the name implies, sipping and blowing through the straw caused her chair to go forward, backward, and turn left or right. This was another challenging feat that she was determined to accomplish.

Finally, on March 16, almost three months after the accident, Mom was discharged from Shepherd Center. Because they did not own a van that could transport Mom, she arrived home by ambulance, greeted by family and friends.

Chapter 8

The New Abnormal

The early days at home were filled with sleepless nights, ventilator emergencies, and a clogged feeding tube, among many other issues. Dad went back to work during the day, and Susan was the primary daytime caregiver. Todd and Dad helped at night, and Dad was the overnight caregiver. Because there was no bedroom on the first floor of the house, the tiny dining room became their bedroom. Mom had to be in a hospital bed on a special air mattress. There wasn't room for a bed for Dad as Mom's care required plenty of space around her bed for the Hoyer lift, the wheelchair, and for her caregivers to move about. The solution was to keep a twin mattress stored against a wall in the kitchen. Once he was finally able to lie down after Mom's bedtime routine each night, Dad would slide the mattress into the dining room next to her bed. Dad got very little sleep as he had to get up multiple times during the night to care for Mom, giving her sips of water, pushing medications into her feeding tube, turning her to keep her from getting pressure sores, adjusting ventilator settings, helping her cough, and so many other things.

Quadriplegia is a nightmare. It is the worst form of physical suffering I have witnessed. Mom also had to deal with phantom pains and sensations. She was often tortured with the sensation that her arm or leg was hanging off the bed or floating in the air. We had to spend time reassuring her of where her limbs were. She would even ask us to show her, so we would raise her leg or arm and then gently lower it again. Then there were the spasms. Multiple times every day, her muscles would spasm, causing her entire body to convulse for a few seconds. Spinal cord injury is traumatic for the brain as it can no longer send and receive messages to the rest of the body properly.

Early on, through their church, Dad sent out a call for help, looking for volunteers who could help Susan with the morning routine, as well as other times during the day when multiple caregivers were needed. The realization that many more helping hands would be needed in the long-term was beginning to settle in. Mom's dear friend from the Cleveland years, Susan Wolters, who is a registered nurse, flew in to help for about a week. She was a huge help, but she now lived in Maine and could not be in Atlanta full-time.

Quite a few women from the church and friends from their neighborhood answered the call for help, regularly working alongside Susan in the mornings. The help provided by Kellie, Terri, and a whole team of neighbors was invaluable. The church was a constant source of support. Every week upon leaving church, there was a homemade meal ready for the family to take home from the church refrigerator. Others also provided meals. One precious volunteer, Laurel, was a seamstress, and she sewed beautiful warm capes for Mom to wear. Mom was constantly miserably cold as a result of her injury. To make the process of dressing Mom easier, Laurel also cut all her shirts up the back and sewed soft seams.

The morning routine took hours and involved administering necessary medications, feeding Mom breakfast, and caring for the ventilator, colostomy, and catheter. Then there was the tedious but necessary wound care. Upon arriving home, a very large wound was discovered on the back of Mom's head, due to that part of her head always being against her pillow or wheelchair headrest. Then bathing, skin care, and her stretching routine all had to happen before getting her dressed and up in her wheelchair for the day. Volunteers then did several loads of laundry each morning and remade her bed after checking the mattress settings. The meals brought by so many proved to be a tremendous blessing, as those caring for Mom were just too busy and exhausted to cook meals.

Those first few months at home, Mom was sick and unstable as her body was still adjusting to the trauma of her injury. She was admitted to the hospital several times for urinary tract infections, blood loss from her colon, and a large abdominal abscess that needed to be drained. In addition to all these problems, a pressure sore was soon discovered on her bottom.

Because Mom was on a ventilator, her stay always had to be in the ICU when she was at the hospital. And because all her care was so specific, a caregiver had to always be with her, which was exhausting for them.

We went back to Atlanta during one of Mom's stays in the ICU. One of the great griefs of her heart was being so isolated. Since she had to be in the ICU, she was not able to see her grandchildren. A dear nurse was very moved by Mom's longing to see her grandchildren. She asked for special permission for the children to visit her, but this was denied, since young children were not allowed in the ICU. So she sneaked us up a back staircase and into Mom's room with our little ones. The joy on Mom's face was so sweet when she saw little Emily, William, and Luke. Those few precious minutes of hugs and kisses from grandchildren did so much to lift Mom's spirits.

During this time, the long-term financial needs were becoming apparent. In addition to the faithful volunteers, we were going to need to hire regular caregivers. Also, anytime Mom needed to leave the house, she had to be transported by either ambulance or a hired van service. A customized van was going to be a necessity. Covenant Presbyterian Church in Cleveland, Mississippi, held fundraisers to raise money toward a van. The Clayton State Laker Angels held a benefit concert. Members of the church in Fayetteville organized golf tournaments. Family, friends, and churches gave generously.

In late spring, the Lord sent the first paid caregiver to our family. Elizabeth Rogers had been referred to us through someone in the church. She had been caregiving for a couple of people, and one of them had recently died. She was still working for her other patient in the mornings, and then she began to take care of Mom from noon until 10:00 p.m. We had no idea at the time what a long-term blessing Elizabeth would be to our family, and that she would in fact become family to us. Alongside Susan, Todd, Dad, and the volunteers, Elizabeth took excellent care of Mom and quickly grew to love her. It did not take long for all of us to come to love her.

Early on, Dad and Susan learned that this was the best way to find good caregivers. Referrals from friends and word of mouth brought more capable hands than going through home health agencies. While these agencies are capable of providing good care for many, we found that they did not have specialized training to care for someone with needs as great and specific as Mom's. We also found that there were many restrictions about what they could and could not do for clients.

Several times early on, Dad hired from these agencies, and it never lasted long. Some found Mom's condition too overwhelming, and others were not loving and did a halfway job of caring for her. There were some who refused to do anything except sit by her side and occasionally intervene in her care. They said they were only allowed to deal with the patient, which meant that they would not be able to contribute in any other way. The daily tasks were monumental to say the least, and the family really needed people who could also do things such as change sheets on her bed, clean trach equipment, and organize medications and supplies, to name only a few.

As summer approached, Mom was reaching milestones while still dealing with very serious issues. Dad was able to begin renting an accessible van while Mom's custom van was being built, and on Mother's Day, he was able to get her to church for the first time since the accident in December.

The pressure sores on her head and bottom were still serious. Due to the severity of the sore on her bottom, Mom was not allowed to be up in her chair for more than two hours at a time. This was very difficult on her, and it also increased the work for her caregivers. Several transfers between the bed and wheelchair each day, in addition to wound care, made for long, exhausting days.

Shepherd Center contacted Dad about Mom being screened for a diaphragm, or phrenic, pacemaker. This would involve surgery to attach an electrode to the phrenic nerve. This device would send energy to the phrenic nerve, which would then cause the diaphragm to expand and contract. If effective, it would allow Mom to be off the ventilator at times. This would be beneficial to her health as it would offer a more natural breathing, unlike the forced breathing on the ventilator. Mom passed the screening tests, but she would need to stay free of infection and other complications and setbacks leading up to this surgery.

By the end of the summer, a plastic surgeon determined that surgery was necessary for the pressure sore on Mom's bottom. Weeks of treatment with a wound vac would be needed to prepare the site for surgery.

In the midst of all the sadness, we had some sweet family news. Susan and I were both expecting babies in March. I was thrilled that God was giving us a fourth child, but I was also experiencing the sad reality that this little one would never be swept up and hugged by his Gram. And for my dear sister, this was her first child, so the joy of pregnancy and the sorrow of Mom's situation were so much greater for her.

Chapter 9

Hope from a Fellow Quadriplegic and Angels

When September came, nine months after the accident, we were still shell-shocked, grieving, and weary. The denomination we are a part of, the Presbyterian Church in America (PCA), hosted the Women in the Church convention in Atlanta. Some friends from our new church in Nashville were planning to go. We also had some dear family friends who planned to attend, and they wanted to visit Mom while they were in town. I was able to get away, which was no small feat, arranging childcare back at home for our three young children.

A long-time family friend, Paige Benton Brown, was one of the speakers, and it was great to get to spend time with the Benton family. Joni Eareckson Tada was also a conference speaker. After the accident, Mom and Dad had been introduced to Joni through a mutual friend, and Joni had sent Mom some emails to encourage her. Joni is also a quadriplegic and is close to Mom's age. She was paralyzed at the age of seventeen due to a diving accident almost forty years earlier.

Since Joni would be traveling from California to Atlanta to speak at the conference, this mutual friend arranged for Mom and our family and friends to meet Joni. Lunch was brought into a private room, where Joni and her caregivers were gracious enough to spend an hour and a half of their time with Mom, Dad, Susan, me, and a few family friends.

I had been impacted by Joni's autobiography when I was a teenager, so talking to her about her hope in the midst of suffering was a blessing. She talked about how difficult life is as a quad, with the constant pain and being completely dependent on others for care. And she shared with us her hope in Christ.

I remember her saying that our society cannot deal with suffering. We run from it, and we are so surprised by it when it comes. She said that we should not be surprised because Jesus said it would happen. She shared John 16:33: "In this world you *will* have trouble. But take heart! I have overcome the world" (NIV). This verse has stayed with me, and the Lord has brought it to mind many times since then.

Soon after Mom's injury, a friend had given me Joni's book, *When God Weeps*. It is a wonderful book, but at the time I lacked the concentration to finish most books. The title alone was enough to minister to me. Knowing that Jesus weeps over our sufferings, like he did at the tomb of his friend Lazarus, was a great comfort.

Just twenty-four hours before Mom's accident, my children had received some books from Mom and Dad for Christmas. They were volumes one and two of *Hymns for a Kid's Heart*, written by Joni Eareckson Tada and Bobbie Wolgemuth. Inside the cover was a note written by Mom to our children. It is the last piece of Mom's handwriting I have, and it is a precious gift. It says, "Christmas 2005. To Emily, William and Luke, I hope you will learn all of these hymns and keep them in your heart where they will always be yours. With love, Gram and Grandpop." When we received this gift, we had no idea that the next day, Mom would become a quadriplegic, just as the author of those books had many years ago.

I learned an important lesson from Joni that day. Upon wheeling into our meeting room, she immediately pulled her wheelchair right up next to Mom's. When she was as close as she could get, she reached over with her frail hand and put it on top of Mom's hand. At that moment, I saw one of the most beautiful smiles I had seen on my mom's face since the accident.

You see, while the bundle of nerves in the spinal cord that controls movement had been catastrophically damaged, the nerves controlling feeling still had enough function that Mom could feel someone holding her hand. Each time someone reached out to hold her hand, it brought her great joy, as well as a feeling of being connected. It was not just that her eyes saw someone holding her hand, she actually felt it. There were occasions when I sat next to Mom as she dozed, her eyes closed. I reached out to put my hand on hers and gently stroked it. Her eyes would open, and she would smile, looking at our hands.

Physical touch is important to all of us. It is a reminder that we are not alone. It makes us feel connected and important to another human being. Sometimes we are afraid to approach those with disabilities and special needs, much less reach out and give a hug, a touch on the shoulder, or a handshake. Admittedly, before Mom's injury, I was often intimidated by the thought of approaching a person with a disability, so I understood why some were afraid to approach or touch her.

Mom did have an intimidating appearance in her large, motorized wheelchair with her ventilator and all the other tubes and bags that were attached to her and her chair, keeping her alive. Quadriplegia can be an extremely isolating condition. The quadriplegic cannot move toward another person but desperately longs for connection with others.

Mom was understanding of and patient with people who seemed nervous around her. But on the occasions that people did approach her with a hug, a kiss on the cheek, or a hand on hers, she beamed, her smile lighting up the room. It made her feel included, seen, and loved.

We left that day knowing Mom had a new friend, a fellow quadriplegic who understood some of what Mom went through on a daily basis. Joni invited Mom to join her email group, a group of quadriplegics from all over the world who communicated with one another, offering encouragement and prayer; a society of suffering that no one would ever voluntarily join.

*****

In early November, the wound site was finally ready, and Mom was able to have the skin flap surgery on the pressure sore site. After a few days in the hospital, Mom was put in isolation when it was discovered she had developed MRSA, a serious staph infection of the blood. She was also showing signs of depression.

Our family was able to go to Atlanta for Thanksgiving, and precious church friends included our family for Thanksgiving dinner. We were able to visit Mom in the hospital while we were in town, but due to the MRSA, we all had to wear gowns and gloves.

In early December, after a month in the hospital, Mom was able to go home. And now that they had an accessible van, Dad, Susan, Elizabeth, and others were able to take Mom Christmas shopping. She had always loved shopping for the perfect gifts for others, so it was such a joy for her to be able to get out and do this herself.

Our family spent Christmas in Jackson with Will's family. We had a sweet time together, but I had a difficult time as I was often preoccupied with the events of Christmas Day the year before.

By early January, Mom was hospitalized again due to a resistant urinary tract infection. Infections were causing her to be anxious and very confused and disoriented.

I was able to travel to visit her during this time. When I walked into the room to see her, she was smiling and talking about things she was seeing in the room, things no one else could see. She directed my attention to a window and told me to look at the crystals. She was trying to tell me the meaning behind them. Mom also told me that my little Luke had been there prophesying. She asked me about Will's retirement and Emily's postdoctoral studies. It was so bizarre to me that she knew her family members' names but her mind was traveling to future decades.

It was during this hospital stay that something very unusual and unexpected happened; an occurrence that was not a hallucination. A dear couple from church visited Mom late one evening in the ICU. The young man prayed over Mom and asked God to send angels into her room. They soon heard whispering behind them. When they finished praying, they looked behind them to see what appeared to be a family with young children, and it sounded as if they were praying in

Spanish. The man had his hands in the air and held a Bible, and the woman had tears running down her cheeks. Very quickly, the family was gone. Shaken, the young couple inquired at the nurses' station about other visitors that evening. Children were not allowed in the ICU, and the nurses said that no one else had been on the floor.

God moves in mysterious ways, and I wonder if these were angels that appeared, or if the Lord allowed them to see some members of the "cloud of witnesses" talked about by the author of Hebrews. Did God pull back the veil between here and eternity for just a moment, so that this couple and Mom could see that we are not alone? There are times in worship that I can almost sense that there are other souls present besides the ones that I can see with my eyes. I believe this is God's kindness in reminding us that we are surrounded by those who are already with him on the other side of the veil.

Chapter 10

Postpartum Depression and Anger

On March 6, 2007, Caleb David Mayfield arrived through an event-ful delivery. We had scheduled an induction ten days before my due date. Because Will's parents lived seven hours away, we wanted to be sure Grandmother would be here to help with our other three children.

During the last few weeks of the pregnancy, Caleb flipped every week, so my doctor kept a close eye on things, performing weekly ultrasounds. The day before the induction, Caleb was in position for delivery. But I woke up at midnight in extreme pain as he flipped again and was now in the breech position. We went into the hospital at five thirty and were offered the choice of either a C-section or an external version. We chose the external route, and it was successful. Caleb had issues with his heart rate throughout the day, and we were so thankful when he arrived safely.

We were thankful to have Will's mother with us to meet Caleb and to care for Emily, William, and Luke. She was wonderful to us, cooking meals, doing laundry, playing games and doing crafts with the kids, and loving us well. But my heart also ached for my mom to be here to meet and to hold her new grandson. The night before Mom Mayfield left to go home, Emily threw up all night long. My dear mother-in-law was up all night long washing bedding and tak-ing care of her. My sweet friend Penny Clarke was planning to come to be with us for the second week. Because Emily had a stomach bug, through sobs, I called Penny and told her we did not think she should come. We would have hated for her to catch the bug and take it home to her family.

We said goodbye to Grandmother that morning, and I felt so alone and overwhelmed to be taking care of four little ones alone while Will worked long days. In addition to his regular work hours and call schedule, he had multiple additional roles in leadership. While I was very proud of him and his leadership abilities, it meant that he had early-morning and late-night meetings several times a month. He served on the hospital board and was chief of surgery at the hospital. He would eventually go on to serve a term as chief of staff and eventually a second term as chief of surgery. Because Will worked so hard outside the home to provide for our growing family and I was a stay-at-home mom, I really felt it was my duty to take care of everything on my own. I very rarely asked for help, and I certainly did not let close friends or even Will know just how over-whelmed I was.

Our church was wonderful, providing meals and visits for us. But most of my friends at church were pregnant or also had new-borns. I had many of the same feelings of despair and depression I had had after delivering William. I was still struggling with such grief over Mom, and now I had postpartum issues to add to the mix. During the previous struggle with this, I never mentioned it to my doctor, and I did not mention it this time either. I was just too ashamed. After Mom's accident, a close friend suggested I might consider going to counseling. I balked at this each time she mentioned it, saying it could not fix Mom's situation. It would be pointless. No one in my family had ever been to counseling, and as far as I knew, no one had ever taken medication for depression. I thought counseling was for people who were really messed up, and I was not.

I was angry with God for Mom's suffering, not only for what it was doing to her but also for what it was doing to our family. I mostly kept it in, but there were times I verbalized it to others. There were times I retreated and withdrew, often through reading. There were cozy books I revisited several times as an escape.

I was so angry and depressed, but there were sweet times when I felt the gentle whisper of God, and these were usually during worship. During the singing, I was often teary, the lump in my throat so big I could not even sing. I was thankful to have a newborn in church with me, as it often gave me the opportunity to leave my pew and stand at the back.

One particular Sunday, I remember standing at the back of the sanctuary, swaying and soothing a fussy Caleb in my arms. We were singing the hymn "Jesus, I Am Resting, Resting," and all I could do was cry, tears streaming down my face as I rocked my baby boy.

> Jesus, I am resting, resting in the joy of what thou art;
> I am finding out the greatness of thy loving heart.
> Thou hast bid me gaze upon thee, as thy beauty fills my soul,
> For by thy transforming power, thou hast made me whole.
> O how great thy lovingkindness, vaster, broader than the sea!
> O how marvelous thy goodness lavished all on me!
> Yes, I rest in thee, Beloved, know what wealth of grace is thine,
> Know thy certainty of promise and have made it mine.
> Simply trusting thee, Lord Jesus, I behold thee as thou art,
> And thy love, so pure, so changeless, satisfies my heart;
> Satisfies its deepest longings, meets, supplies its ev'ry need,
> Compasseth me round with blessings: thine is love indeed.
> Ever lift thy face upon me as I work and wait for thee;

Resting 'neath thy smile, Lord Jesus, earth's dark
    shadows flee.
Brightness of my Father's glory, sunshine of my
    Father's face,
Keep me ever trusting, resting, fill me with thy
    grace.

(Jean Sophia Pigott, 1876)

The words of this beautiful hymn have ministered to me many times, reminding me to gaze at Jesus and to find my rest in him.

When Caleb was a few weeks old, Will's parents returned to Nashville to celebrate his baptism. It was a bittersweet occasion. Both my parents and Will's parents had been with us to celebrate the baptisms of our three older children. Because of Mom's condition, she and Dad were unable to come.

A couple of weeks after Caleb was born, my sister became a mom for the first time. Mary Evelynn Brown, beautiful and healthy, came into the world on her momma's birthday. We were soon able to go to Atlanta to meet her, and Mom, Dad, and Susan's family were able to meet newborn Caleb as well. Mom loved having those two tiny babies in her lap in her wheelchair, but it also grieved her that she could not pick them up and hold them with her own arms.

Even though she had a newborn, Susan continued to be Mom's primary daytime caregiver. It was an extremely difficult balance to simultaneously care for her new baby girl and Mom's constant life-and-death needs. Even though there were often other caregivers with Susan, she was sometimes the only one there who was trained to take care of Mom's ventilator needs. There were times Susan had to put down a screaming baby in the middle of nursing because Mom had a ventilator emergency.

Because of the life-and-death nature of Mom's condition, someone who was trained in how to operate her ventilator had to be with her twenty-four hours a day. The problem we were having was that caregivers were very nervous at the thought of being left alone with Mom. But over time, after having cared for Mom for some time, several were ready and willing to learn. When Mary Evelynn was six months old, Susan and Todd moved out of Mom and Dad's house and into one of their own. Susan was still the primary daytime caregiver, so she and the baby still spent most days at Mom and Dad's.

Caregiving for a family member in extreme circumstances takes a toll on a family, and our family was no exception. Many were the times we grew frustrated and even angry with each other. And because hired caregivers and volunteers were always with us, they often felt the tension and were a part of it. We are forever indebted to these dear people who put up with so much and continued to love and care for not only Mom but for all of us!

*****

Because of the nature of Will's work and frequent weekends on call, I sometimes loaded up all four kids and made the trip to Atlanta without him. Those were exhausting trips, but I knew I needed to spend time with Mom and Dad.

On one of these trips without Will, Dad quietly knocked on my door in the middle of the night, saying, "Jules, I really need your help with Mom. Something's happened." I quickly dressed and went downstairs to find that Mom's ostomy bag had ruptured and that she was covered in her own stool. I thought, *Really, Lord? As if her condition isn't already enough, how can you allow things like this? She's covered in her own filth!* Caleb was still little at the time, so I prayed that he would not wake up while Dad and I worked. Through tears, Dad and I spent probably two hours cleaning Mom. It was everywhere. She slept off and on while we worked. Occasionally, she would wake and want to know what was wrong and what we were doing. We calmly reassured her, and she would rest again.

All while she lay in bed, we changed her sheets under her and meticulously bathed her entire torso and legs. And I thought about how completely helpless she was, paralyzed and lying in her filth. She could do nothing to help us clean her.

It reminds me of the fact that we are completely helpless to make ourselves clean before God. We are paralyzed. In fact, the Bible says in Ephesians 2 that we were dead in our trespasses and sins. Dead.

Ephesians 2:1–9 says,

> And you were dead in the trespasses and sins in which you once walked, following the course of this world, following the prince of the power of the air, the spirit that is now at work in the sons of disobedience—among whom we all once lived in the passions of our flesh, carrying out the desires of the body and the mind, and were by nature children of wrath, like the rest of mankind. But God, being rich in mercy, because of the great love with which he loved us, even when we were dead in our trespasses, made us alive together with Christ—by grace you have been saved—and raised us up with him and seated us with him in the heavenly places in Christ Jesus, so that in the coming ages he might show the immeasurable riches of his grace in kindness toward us in Christ Jesus. For by grace you have been saved through faith. And this is not your own doing; it is the gift of God, not a result of works, so that no one may boast. (ESV)

Just as all Mom could do was lie there and let me and Dad clean her, this is our posture before our heavenly Father. We are completely helpless, lying in our own filthy sin. He cleanses us and breathes life into us. We do nothing to contribute to our salvation.

Chapter 11

The Collision of Joy and Sorrow

As sad as Mom's condition was, we enjoyed some sweet times when we were together. When Mom had to be in bed for extended periods of time during the day due to pressure sores, the grandchildren would crawl into bed with her to snuggle and watch movies. They would read to her, and when she was up in her chair, they would crawl into her lap. Luke spent a lot of time sitting in Mom's lap. When we went on outings, he quite often wanted to ride through stores and into church in her lap. We were so grateful God gave us sweet moments like these in the midst of grief and sadness.

We had many visits from friends and extended family who would stop by as they traveled through Atlanta: Johnna, Elisabeth, Wilson, Pam, Bill, Susan, and many others from our Mississippi years. My Uncle Larry and Aunt Barbara came from Pennsylvania at least once a year. We were there for one of those visits. My sweet Aunt Barb brought fun cookie cutters with her, and she made cookies with my children as Mom looked on from her wheelchair. This may not seem special, but to me it was a beautiful display of love toward Mom, my children, and me. Because Mom was now disabled, Aunt Barb was being my mom's hands with her grandchildren.

Before Mom's injury, she mentored many young women and teenagers, and she loved encouraging others. Although it looked much different after her injury, she continued to love others well from her wheelchair. She often spent one-on-one time with her caregivers, listening to their struggles and offering encouragement. One year early after her accident, it was her idea to host an annual Christmas party for all her caregivers. She would plan the menu and have it catered, and have gifts placed at each caregiver's place at the table. Everyone in the house would take a short break from the daily routine to enjoy time together around the table.

Marty and Denise, friends of Mom and Dad's from church, were often the hands and feet of Jesus to our family. Marty loves to cook, and he is an excellent cook. He also knew that before the accident, Mom and Dad loved to regularly have people at their home for meals.

Because they wanted Mom and Dad to be able to continue to show hospitality to others, Marty and Denise took it upon themselves to cook a full meal at Mom and Dad's house on a regular basis. They encouraged Mom and Dad to invite anyone they wanted, and once they knew the number of people, they planned the meal. These dear friends arrived early each time, lugging heavy coolers and other containers full of food and cooking supplies. Right there in Mom and Dad's kitchen, they transformed the ingredients into a delicious meal while visiting with Mom and Dad, the caregivers, and the invited guests once they arrived.

We had the blessing of being the recipients of one of these fabulous meals prepared by Marty and Denise on one of our visits. What a beautiful gift their service was to Mom and Dad and to all of us!

All the while, Mom's caregivers continued to become an extended family for us. They were part of holidays and birthday celebrations, as well as the normal everyday moments, like playing outside on warm days while Mom sat and watched from her chair. They were so patient with our little children, who often ran in and out of Mom's room and played underfoot during her morning routine.

One of my favorite memories is of one of those days when we were all resting and watching a movie together. Elizabeth and three-year-old Luke were snuggling together on the sofa. Luke looked at her and said, "Liz, are you chocolate?" And then, he licked her arm! She laughed so hard, and said, "I don't know, Luke, are you vanilla?" We all laughed and laughed, and I thought it was beautiful that he had known her for a couple years before he really noticed that her skin was a different color from his.

Humor became a tremendous gift and stress reliever. We relished stories told by Liz and other caregivers, and laughed around the firepit at night while Dad told the kids funny, scary stories. Because there were so many technical terms surrounding Mom's care, even humor related to her care became important. At some point, caregivers named Mom's ostomy bag "Harry," and her catheter and urine bag became known as "Cathy." The names stuck.

Later that year, in September, we were blessed with another niece, as Jeff and Wendy welcomed Lexi Lynn.

In October of 2007, Mom had another health scare when caregivers noticed some swelling around her abdomen. Because she had had ovarian cancer just two years earlier, her doctor ordered a CAT scan. It showed several concerning issues, including a new L5 spine fracture, a large kidney stone, and some fluid on the abdomen.

The cause of the fracture was unknown, and there was nothing that could be done about it. The abdominal fluid, though, had to be drained and tested for cancer cells. We were all thankful and relieved to find out that the fluid tested negative. With all Mom's health issues from the paralysis, her body probably could not have handled more chemotherapy and radiation.

As Mom eventually stabilized, more opportunities arose for her. For one, she was able to get out of the house several times a week. Caregivers and family were able to take her shopping, to see movies, and out to eat. Bob Lindley often drove a van full of ladies, including his wife, Anne, around town on shopping excursions. These were always massive efforts, but they were good for Mom and her caregivers, enabling them to have some fun and a change of scenery.

After the accident, Mom obviously was unable to continue in her role as the children's ministry director at their church, so her dear friend Sue Jakes was hired to direct the ministry. One Christmas, Sue asked Mom to help her with getting the children's Christmas program together. At one of their meetings, she told Mom, "Well, Lynn, we're quite a pair! You can't move, and I can't sing, but together maybe we can pull this off!"

Mom had always enjoyed watching games on television, and after they moved to Atlanta, she especially enjoyed cheering for the Braves, sometimes going to games. So, of course, after the accident, watching games on television from her bed or wheelchair became a favorite pastime. David and Debbie Epps, also fans, went with Mom and Dad to several games. On one occasion, Mom even got to meet a favorite player.

Of course, these outings always drew attention. On one of these occasions, as we were eating at Truett's, a full-table-service Chick-fil-A, with a rather large group of family and caregivers, we asked our waiter for the check. He told us that it had been taken care of by someone who had been moved by watching our family as we ate with Mom. We asked who it was because we wanted to thank them, but he said they were already gone. They had left the restaurant in tears, he said. Being recipients of this act of kindness and many others like it was always very humbling. These events were also great teaching opportunities as we shared and talked about them with our children.

*****

In the spring of 2008, Mom developed shingles. For me, this was another moment of asking God how much more she could take. Here she was, paralyzed from the neck down, and the shingles sores were around her lips, where she could feel them. It was extremely painful for her, and it caused extreme, long-term sensitivity on that side of her face.

Around this time, our church in Nashville was doing a ladies' luncheon series, and they asked Mom to be one of the speakers, via video. Mom meticulously and thoughtfully planned her talk, with the help of her caregivers taking notes for her and helping her look up Scriptures.

Then, on a weekend visit in Atlanta, we recorded her talk. I sat on a stool next to Mom in their cozy little living room, the flames gently dancing in the fireplace behind us. Recording a twenty-minute talk was a daunting undertaking for Mom and for everyone involved.

Dad operated the video camera. Caregivers watched and played with my four little children and kept them quiet.

Mom did the speaking; her voice was weak and quiet, and her words were very difficult to understand. When it came to the Scripture passages, I read those aloud with her. Being on a ventilator, Mom only had a few seconds to speak on each inhale. For the few seconds of the exhale, she was unable to make a sound; she would often continue to try to speak, but no sound came. Every five seconds, the ventilator made a terrible noise, which was very loud and similar to a small foghorn.

Multiple times, we stopped the camera to take care of Mom. She needed water, her weight-shift timer went off, and she also just needed some breaks, as the process was very taxing on her. She was clearly not feeling well, and she was in terrible pain throughout the process. We also stopped the recording to help with the kids when they struggled to stay quiet in the small house. Then, once everyone was settled, we started the recording where Mom had left off.

At home the next week, I played through the video and wrote down a transcript of every word Mom said in the talk. Many times, I had to rewind to understand what she said in places and also to lip-read in those places she had spoken on the exhale and there was no sound. But for the most part, she spoke so slowly that it was not too difficult.

When I had completed the transcript, I sat down at the computer with Will while he painstakingly captioned her words on the screen to match the video. I was so grateful for his willingness to do this, as it would aid so greatly in people being able to understand Mom.

In April, the day of the luncheon arrived, and I was a nervous wreck. Mom had asked me to speak to the ladies to introduce her as the speaker, as well as to tell the story of the accident. I did so, and I sobbed through a good bit of it. We handed out the outline of her talk with the Scripture references prepared by her caregivers, then the recorded video of Mom's talk was played.

At one point in the video, Mom said that people ask her all the time how she can stand this, and they tell her that she is ministering to them. Her explanation to this was, "It's because Christ is ministering to me at the same time. My ministry to others is in his strength, not mine." She also said, "If I could only do one thing in this lesson, it would be to encourage you to memorize Scripture and put it in your heart. One of my favorite and first memories after the accident was when I first woke up, and they told me what had happened. Right away, that verse, 'All of the days ordained were meant to be...' I just thought right away, *This is your day too, Lord.*"

There were other times Mom had the opportunity to speak to church groups, and people were blessed by her testimony.

Chapter 12

Anniversaries and Milestones

In June of 2008, my parents and Will's parents celebrated their fortieth wedding anniversaries. They had been married one week apart in June of 1968, and Will and I knew what a blessing it was that both sets of parents had been together this long.

For several months leading up to my parents' anniversary, my siblings and I were making plans for a surprise party for my parents. We mailed invitations to family and friends near and far. We also asked them to send letters for Mom and Dad to me ahead of time. I compiled these in a photo album, along with wedding pictures and family memories from over the years.

Our three families came together with Mom and Dad for the weekend. Before we arrived, we told them that we had scheduled some time with a photographer for a family portrait. We coordinated clothing ahead of time; it was a great way to secretly also get them dressed for the surprise party.

After the portrait, we headed to the church, where family and friends were waiting to celebrate with them. They were so surprised. It was a very emotional time for Mom. In attendance were extended family and her college roommate from Pennsylvania, friends from Mississippi, our pastor and his wife from our summers in Colorado, and, of course, local friends. We presented my parents with the memory book. It was a wonderful afternoon of celebration. It was a precious gift that Mom was still alive to see this milestone.

Not long after that, our family, along with Will's brothers' families, descended upon Jackson to celebrate their parents' fortieth anniversary. Mom Mayfield had arranged babysitters at the house for all the grandchildren, and we took them out to a lovely celebration dinner at Amerigo.

It was a busy, full summer for Mom and Dad. In July, Terry Starr and many other friends at Covenant Presbyterian in Fayetteville organized a golf tournament to help raise money for Mom's mounting expenses.

One Sunday before the tournament, as Mom and Dad arrived in the church sanctuary, they were surprised to see a video message from their friend and fellow quadriplegic Joni Eareckson Tada encouraging Mom's friends to support the golf tournament. What a surprise! And what a kind thing of Joni to do for Mom and Dad.

More excitement happened for Mom that summer, as she had her first trip to the beach since her injury. Mom had always loved the beach, and Dad did not know if he would ever be able to get her there again. But they loaded up the trailer with all Mom's supplies and spent two nights at Hilton Head, where they were able to wheel Mom out onto the beach on an accessible walkway. Caregivers Elizabeth and Leah went along with them, putting in long, fourteen-hour days caring for Mom. Susan and Mary Evelynn were able to go too.

Late in the summer of 2008, Mom received the gift of her first eye-gaze computer, through the generosity of Jeff and Wendy. Up until then, Mom had benefited somewhat from voice-recognition software. This program was similar to what Will used for dictation at work. However, because Mom's voice was so weak, it proved to be very tedious and ineffective for her.

Dad had learned about a company in the country that produced the eye-gaze computer and software. They were a husband-and-wife team located in Virginia, and they traveled to Atlanta to do setup and training with Mom and Dad.

It was quite astounding that Mom could learn to use her eyes to run the computer. Each time she sat at the computer, she stared at a device that then calibrated her computer to respond to her gaze.

This became a huge blessing for Mom going forward. Early on, she learned to do some basic tasks, such as playing Connect Four. This was a favorite of the grandchildren, who would take turns sitting in a chair next to her to play the game together. William especially loved this time with Gram. Later, as she grew more skilled and accustomed to using it, she was able to email, shop online, and surf the Internet, all independently.

Mom had always enjoyed reading, and in her condition, it was very difficult to read a book. It was hard to get the book at the right angle and distance, and someone had to turn each page. Dad was eventually able to set up her Kindle to feed to her computer screen. Now she was able to read independently, using her eyes to turn each page.

Since the day of the accident, Dad had sent out regular updates on Mom's condition. On August 19, 2008, Mom sent out an update. The following email was composed and typed independently, using her eyes.

Subject: Hello from Lynn

Hi to all of our faithful family and friends,

This is a letter that I am typing using my eyes and my eye-gaze computer.

God is so good all of the time.

If I were to list all of the good gifts sent to us from our heavenly Father, it would be impossible. He has used His people in such a variety of ways that truly I stand in amazement as I watch Him work. I'm not good at long letters, but I want to express my love and thanks to you for your love, care, time, encouragement, laughter, tears, meals and much more.

News items:

> We've been working hard on this new computer. Elizabeth has been a wonderful help. Susan and Mary Evelynn are back with us, what a joy. Today is Leah's birthday and she recently graduated from Clayton State. Tomorrow we will head to the hospital to get my feeding tube replaced. This is usually a quick procedure, which is good since the hospital is not a favorite place of mine.
> I think my eyes are telling me it is time to stop.
>
> With much love,
> Lynn

"Whate'er my God ordains is right."
This sits above my computer
where I can see it daily.

The above email is truly remarkable, given that it was written by someone who was paralyzed from the neck down, could not breathe on her own, and could only use her eyes to compose an email to communicate in this way. Technology is amazing!

*****

Our family continued to grow on both sides! Early in 2009, Todd and Susan welcomed Isabella, and Penny was born to Nick and Tanya. We loved having these nieces and nephews, and it was so fun watching our parents with all these grandchildren.

Another sweet time was the celebration of Emily's tenth birthday in the fall of 2009. I took Emily to Atlanta where we had a precious birthday lunch at the American Girl Store bistro with all four of her grandparents and Mom's caregivers. She loved shopping around the store with both of her grandmothers, and her grandfathers were such good sports!

Chapter 13

A Necessary Trial in Court

Within days of Mom's accident in 2005, an investigator went to look at the damaged vehicle that Mom had been riding in. He noticed that Mom's seat had broken away from the body of the car. A mutual friend of his approached Dad with this information and asked if it would be all right to buy the car before it was destroyed so that he could do further research. Dad agreed, although he did not want to sue anyone. On the other hand, if the vehicle manufacturer was negligent, he wanted to help to prevent future catastrophic injuries to others, and he also needed to be able to care for Mom for the rest of her life.

Eventually an attorney was hired. After many months of research and investigation of the vehicle, it was determined that the latch that secured Mom's seat to the body of the vehicle had indeed broken. This caused her to strike her head on the console between the two front seats. There was evidence that the company knew this latch was faulty, but they had failed to do anything about it. They also failed to install the safer shoulder belts in the middle back seats, despite decades of research showing that lap-only seat belts are not safe.

So in the months leading up to the trial at the end of 2009, many of us were required to give depositions. Attorneys from both sides of the case came to Nashville to take separate depositions from Will and me. I spent an hour in a hotel conference room describing the scene of the accident and answering questions about that day, and also about how Mom and Dad's life had changed because of it.

When I told them about the wonderful African American man who stopped at the scene, held my sobbing brother in a bear hug, and prayed with him, I was shocked to hear the defense attorney question this. He asked, "Are you sure he was hugging your brother? He may have been restraining Jeff to keep him from getting to the other driver." I could not believe he would twist it like that. I pushed back on that and told him that that dear man was hugging and comforting Jeff.

At the end of the deposition, one of them wanted to know what about Mom's condition had been difficult for me. I shared several obvious things, but I remember very vividly saying, "Seeing my dad so exhausted from taking care of Mom, and knowing that he hasn't slept in a real bed because there's no room for one in their dining room." Up until that point, I had been able to hold it together pretty well, but I began to cry and could not really speak anymore. I went home, completely spent, to relieve my sweet friend and neighbor Rachel Roper, who had come over to take care of our kids while I gave my deposition.

The case against the motor vehicle company finally went to court in December of 2009. Family members who had been at the scene of the accident were called to testify, as well as caregivers and family friends. Mom and Dad also testified.

The motor vehicle company's own crash tests were presented as evidence. In these tests, the rear seat collapsed, causing the crash-test dummies to sustain similar injuries to what Mom had sustained. In spite of these crash tests, the company had moved forward with the manufacturing design.

Of course, Will had to testify. In court cases, often the timing of when each witness is needed can be unpredictable. Will wanted to be able to keep working and taking care of his patients without having to be there in Atlanta, possibly waiting days for his turn to testify. So when Will's day came, the attorneys were able to send a private jet to pick him up from the airport closest to his hospital. This was a huge blessing for him, and we were so grateful for their planning in this.

I hated that I was not allowed to be in the courtroom to support Will. Because of Mom's injury, the defense really grilled him about his care in getting Mom out of the car. They would have liked to have been able to prove that the way he moved her caused further injury. Suspecting the possibility of spinal cord injury when he first saw Mom in the car, he had been very careful to stabilize her head and neck as he moved her.

I had also been asked to testify. I arranged childcare for the children back home, traveled to Atlanta, and spent the day in a holding room with other witnesses. As I entered the holding room, I was shocked. There, all around the room, were large poster-size photos of Mom before the accident. The one etched in my memory is the one of Mom playing in the lake with three-year-old, floaty-clad Emily on her back, huge smiles on both their faces. It was too much to look at. Mom's attorneys were of course using the photos so that the jury could see what Mom had been like before her injury, a visual of what had been lost. So I spent the day along with others in that room, wondering what was going on in the courtroom and trying to keep my eyes from drifting to those images. They never called me to the stand.

In the end, the jury found in favor of Mom and Dad, finding the defense liable for the defects in the vehicle that caused the extent of Mom's injuries. Following the verdict, the jury reconvened to discuss punitive damages. Before they could return with a decision, attorneys for the motor vehicle company decided to settle.

We were grateful that attention was called to these vehicle defects and problems, and that hopefully others would be spared such devastating injuries. Of course, the public nature of this was difficult as it was on the Atlanta area evening news, as well as in print.

At the conclusion of the trial, Mom and Dad were able to speak with the driver of the other car. He had not been intentionally reckless, but because he was at fault, he also had to be present at the trial. He was now a young man with a family of his own. Dad was able to share the gospel with him and offer forgiveness.

*****

We were so grateful that there would be provision for Mom's continued care and needs thanks to the outcome of the suit. The next year, Mom and Dad were finally able to move into a larger house, where Mom would have more room to move about. The house had a downstairs master suite, and the bedroom was large enough for Mom's hospital bed and equipment. The best part about this was that Dad would no longer have to sleep on a rollaway bed or on a mattress on the floor anymore. There was space in their room for Dad to have a real bed. Many nights after Mom was settled in bed for the night, he rolled his bed right next to hers so that he could hold her hand while they watched a Braves game or a movie.

The new house also gave Mom a better space for her eye-gaze computer and desk, where she could enjoy afternoons sending and receiving emails, shopping for gifts online, reading, and playing computer games with her grandchildren.

Mom had always been an encourager, and she really enjoyed the ability to send emails to encourage others, including Joni Eareckson Tada and the group of quadriplegics who kept in touch with one another.

Joni has a radio program, and an email she received from Mom became the topic of her radio program one day early in 2009. She explained how Mom used the eye-gaze software to type with her eyes. Then Joni said, "And Lynn's message that she wrote to me today with her eyes? I can't imagine how long it took for her to write this with that blinking and looking, but she wrote, 'Joni, thank you for taking time to encourage others as you go about your day. You may never know the power of the seed you plant.' I could not believe this woman was thanking *me* for encouraging *her*…I mean, you've gotta know how I felt humbled after I realized Lynn meticulously wrote that with her eye movements."

She went on later in the broadcast to say that she certainly needed to hear a hopeful word that day, and it came from someone so paralyzed she "can't even shrug her shoulders, but I tell you what, she can encourage with her eyes. Not just with the way she smiles with her eyes or looks with her eyes, but the way she types with her eyes!" Then she closed the broadcast by encouraging her listeners to let the Lord give them "words to sustain those around you today and tonight!" (*Joni and Friends* radio broadcast, January 28, 2009).

Chapter 14

A Better Way to Breathe and Breathing Life into Others

During that first year of Mom's injury, she underwent a screening to determine her eligibility for a diaphragm pacemaker. It was decided that she was a good candidate, but there were some problems at the time. In addition to Mom not being healthy and stable enough for the surgery, the only approved surgical approach at the time was through the abdominal area. This was not an option for Mom, due to the massive amounts of scar tissue from her ovarian cancer surgery, radiation, and the surgery following the accident. The only option for her was to go in through her chest.

The summer of 2010, several years after the initial testing for the procedure, Dad received good news. The surgical approach Mom needed had been approved. She had the surgery to install the pacemaker that summer. The surgery was performed by Dr. Saeid Khansarinia, who, according to MDatl.com, was the only surgeon doing the procedure through the chest. Christopher Reeve, the actor who played Superman, had also had this surgery, and the surgeon who had performed his surgery came down to Atlanta to assist with Mom's surgery. Mom became one of the first people to have the surgery done using the new approach through the chest.

Initially, we were told that it can take some patients extended periods of time to work up the stamina to be off the ventilator and on the pacer. Within weeks, however, Mom was spending most of her days on the pacer, which was remarkable! The only exceptions were mealtimes, as she found it to be much more comfortable to be on the ventilator for eating.

Mom, Dad, and all the caregivers found the pacer to be a tremendous blessing. There were significant safety and health benefits for Mom. With the ventilator, there was always a risk of the tubing popping off. This happened sometimes, which was why someone always had to be nearby. Sometimes we noticed, and sometimes Mom got our attention through making clicking noises or whispering as loudly as she could.

Pacing offers a much more natural form of breathing for the patient, as opposed to the forced positive air from the ventilator. This greatly reduces the risk of pneumonia and other problems associated with being on a ventilator.

That same year, Mom was interviewed about her injury by some representatives from Mission to North America. MNA is a division of our denomination, the Presbyterian Church in America. Each year, the Women in the Church of the PCA collects a love gift. In 2010, the love gift focus was for ministries to those with special needs in our churches. Mom was interviewed, videoed, and featured along with others with disabilities. The video was then distributed to churches in the PCA to make them aware of where that year's funds would be going.

In the interview, Mom spoke of the fear she experienced early on in her injury. "Because of the helplessness and inability to communicate, I could only hope that this condition would not be permanent. Everything had changed for me, and I often felt very alone." When asked about the area of life in which she needed the most assistance, she replied, "Emotional support is my greatest need. Fellowship with family and friends is invaluable." She talked about how things like going to church, formerly simple, now took hours of planning and preparation.

She shared about the confusion she had felt as she adjusted to the hard work of living with this disability, and how she had to keep Psalm 139:16 as the focus of her mind through all that was happening to her: "Your eyes saw my unformed body; all the days ordained for me were written in your book before one of them came to be."

Mom said, "I had to learn to eat. I had to learn to talk. And all of this was very hard work. Occasionally my emotions would take a nosedive as the reality of it all set in each day. Spiritually I was okay. I would tell family and friends, 'It is well with my soul.' I was not just saying that to encourage them. It was really true. I also found myself with an ever-increasing longing for heaven; not a desire to die but looking forward to heaven."

When asked, "How have you seen the work of God displayed in your life through disability?" Mom answered, "The opportunity to tell my story is an opportunity to tell his story. Everyone who sees me wants to know what happened, and if they ask, they hear about the God who keeps me. My grandchildren have learned compassion and service as they see it all around me. Watching my journey is to know that God is at work in my life and in lives that touch me each day. When we are weak, he is strong."

The interviewer asked, "How has your local church ushered in the power of the gospel—in word and deed—into your life and the life of your family?" Mom responded, "The gospel is 'God with us,' and our church family is 'with us.' There are volunteers who cook and clean, ladies in our church who share their gifts with us on a regular basis. One of the men in our church learned to drive our special needs van so that he can take me and his wife to run errands and shop. There is a meal prepared for us every Sunday after church, and we know that if we have a need of any kind, the body will make an effort to meet that need."

Mom was also asked, "How does the care of the local church free you or your family members up to minister to others?" Mom answered, "We love to practice hospitality. A man in our church who is an excellent cook regularly prepares a meal in our home so that we can invite friends over for food and fellowship. It was his idea, and it has been a blessing not only to us but also to the many who have been invited for dinner. Most of my life has been spent teaching children, and my disability has not prohibited me from continuing to use my spiritual gifts. I am presently teaching the Shorter Catechism to the older elementary class at my church. I have also taught them the books of the Bible and the Ten Commandments through music and fun activities."

Finally, the interviewer asked, "If you could share one message with the church about the subject of disability, what would it be?" Mom said, "Love those with disabilities like Jesus does. Don't treat them any differently. We are all image bearers who need love and who will love back as the gospel works in and through us." (These excerpts were taken from the MNA SNM interview with Sue Jakes, posted by Stephanie Opdahl Hubach on Lynn Wheeler's Facebook page, in memory of her.)

Chapter 15

Grandparenting in Joy and in Sorrow

In June of 2010, Will and I traveled to San Diego so that he could run the Rock 'n' Roll Marathon there. The kids stayed in Jackson with Will's parents and had a great time doing all the things they loved to do with Grandmother and Pop. They went to VBS, baked, tended the rose garden, played games, and so much more.

Of course, Grandmother had her traditional "sacks" ready for their visit. The sacks were brown paper bags labeled with the days of the week, and they each contained some sort of activity, craft, or a little toy. Each morning of their visit, the kids could not wait to open that day's sack together to find out what they would do with Grandmother and Pop that day! This was a tradition for almost every visit at their house in Jackson.

This was the first time that Will and I really had time away together since having children, and we were so thankful for Mom and Dad's willingness to keep them and to love them so well.

Will's dad had recently been diagnosed with dystonia, and then what the doctors called a "Parkinson's-like condition." He had also developed a tremor in his hand and was no longer doing surgery. He continued to run a full-time ophthalmology clinic, though. He seemed to be doing well, and in January of that year, Mom and Dad had gained another grandson with the birth of Noah to Jenny and Alex.

*****

More running training ensued that year, as Susan and I decided to do our first ever half marathons together. Since Mom had been a runner and had been my first running partner many years earlier, it was a good way for the two of us to work through some grief together. In the fall, we met at Walt Disney World for the inaugural Wine and Dine Half Marathon. It was a late-night race, and crossing the finish line together at 1:00 a.m. was such an emotional experience for us. It was a great couple of days for us, acting like kids again and exploring the parks together.

Because Susan and I had such a great experience running our half marathon at Disney, we thought it would be fun to take our families in January and have our husbands join us for the Disney World Half Marathon. We talked to Mom and Dad about joining us too.

So in January, our family, Susan's family, Mom and Dad, and caregivers Liz and Kristy all made the trek to Orlando. We rented a large house that would be accessible for Mom. Mom and Dad had been quite adventurous, traveling a few times a year to see their grandchildren or go on vacation to the beach. Travel with Mom was quite a process, and involved pulling a trailer loaded with Mom's bed, an extra wheelchair, the Hoyer lift, and countless bins filled with ventilator supplies, medications, and all the other equipment needed to care for her.

Even with the many challenges of caring for Mom in a new place, we had some sweet, magical moments. We got to spend a couple of days together at Magic Kingdom and Hollywood Studios, as well as enjoy shopping at Downtown Disney and fun character meals at Chef Mickey's and 1900 Park Fare. The characters at these meals gave Mom so much attention. Mickey Mouse and Donald Duck kissed her on the cheek, and of course, Prince Charming gave her plenty of attention! Seeing Mom's face as she wheeled down Main Street toward Cinderella Castle was priceless.

The best moment of all was when Mom got to ride "It's a Small World." There are several wheelchair-accessible boats on the attraction. When one of those boats came around, the cast members rolled her onto a boat and locked her wheelchair onto it. We all piled into her boat and the one behind it. The grandchildren loved having Gram on the ride with them. When the ride was over, she told the cast member, "That was the most adventurous I've been since my accident!"

Our kids and their cousins, Mary Evelynn and Isabella, all ran the Disney kids' races. The morning of the half marathon, Susan, Todd, Will, and I left the house at 3:30 a.m. to get to the race. Liz, Kristy, Mom, and Dad took care of the kids while we were running. I am so thankful for the gift of that vacation together and for the memories that were made.

In September of that year, the last Mayfield grandchild was born. Jenny and Alex welcomed little Mason, their fourth baby boy.

*****

The next summer, Will and I had the opportunity to go sailing with friends in the British Virgin Islands. Mom and Dad offered to have the kids come to Atlanta to stay with them, and they felt like they could manage it, with Dad, Susan, Todd, and the caregivers all being available to pitch in. I had a twinge of guilt, however, leaving them with this responsibility, in addition to the enormity of Mom's day-to-day care. But I think these opportunities for Mom and Dad to feel like normal grandparents were very important to them.

The kids had a fun-filled week, spending time with their grandparents, aunt and uncle and cousins, and caregivers, who were like family by this time. Will and I had a wonderful time sailing; at the age of forty-one, it was my first time out of the country.

Chapter 16

The Monumental Task of Starting Over

In the fall of 2012, Susan and Todd received the news that Todd's company would be transferring him to the Alabama coast. Once they moved, this would leave Mom and Dad without family in the area. Since Will had an established medical practice by this point and we likely would not be moving, Mom and Dad decided to move to the Nashville area. This would be a daunting process for them, as Mom would need new doctors, caregivers, and an accessible home.

I spent the end of the year looking at many houses with our dear realtor and friend Susan Kelton. She was so patient with the long list of requirements that Mom and Dad needed in a house. We were able to narrow it down to just a few houses. Mom and Dad came from Atlanta to look, and after getting Mom inside the first house, they made an offer on it.

Mom and Dad made the move to Brentwood in January of 2013. A small army of family, caregivers, and dear friends helped them sort through, organize, and pack for the move. Mom and Dad's dear friends Bob and Anne Lindley traveled with them to help with the move. Our pastor, Ian Sears, brought dinner to feed us all that first night. Over the coming days and weeks, many hands helped unpack boxes, organize Mom's supplies, and take care of many details to help them feel settled in their new home.

Amazingly, Liz and Kristy agreed to move here with them to continue caring for Mom. Dad had hired contractors to turn the large basement into an apartment for them. Very quickly, however, the search began for additional caregivers. I was able to fill in occasionally when needed, but with my family's needs, I was limited in the amount of time I could be available. I had always been afraid of being alone with Mom, but I soon learned how to operate her ventilator and how to take care of possible emergencies.

The move was difficult on all of them at first. Building a new community was not easy. Liz was living away from her husband and son, Kristy was starting over with friendships, and I knew Mom and Dad were lonely and desiring friendship. I was so grateful for our pastor Ian, who visited Mom weekly to encourage her.

One evening, soon after Mom and Dad moved here, the enemy was heaping guilt upon me for not visiting Mom as often as I should. Immediately, the Spirit whispered the verse, "The Lord is near to the brokenhearted and saves the crushed in spirit" (Psalm 34:18 ESV). It reminded me that God is the one who comforts and is near, and it freed me from the guilt of thinking I needed to be near them all the time.

Even though they had to start over completely with finding physicians for Mom, many aspects of this were much easier to navigate than they had been in Atlanta. There, for the most part, they had to drive into large Atlanta hospitals in the downtown area, navigating heavy traffic and parking garages. In the Nashville area, they were able to find doctors to treat her in a smaller hospital only twenty minutes from their house. No heavy traffic, and no parking garages.

Soon after moving to be near us, Mom had some swelling in her leg. Dad took her to see Will, and the X-ray revealed that she had suffered a broken tibia. Thankfully, the bone was fairly stable. Because surgery was so risky for Mom, Will decided against it and put her in a boot for several months instead. Of course, this complicated the daily routines. The caregivers had to be very careful when bathing and moving Mom.

I wondered if I had caused this at some point, and I felt so guilty. In their house, there was a very tricky and tight turn to wheel her out of her bedroom. At least once when I was pushing her chair, unknowingly to me, her foot caught on the corner. I did not see it and I continued to push her chair, realizing too late that her foot was caught.

One of the many aspects of Mom's regular medical care that had always been a source of much anxiety for her was her trach tube change, which happened every few months. In Atlanta, they had to spend most of the day at the hospital, and it was very painful for her. Once they moved to the Nashville area, they found a great pulmonologist to do it in his office. After doing it there the first few times, he asked them where they lived. Upon realizing that he lived close to them, and that their home was on his way to work, he offered to come by the house to do it. This was a huge blessing! It was still a very uncomfortable procedure, but he was very kind to her and did it quickly and efficiently each time.

As he had faithfully done all these years, God soon provided additional caregivers. A professor in our church let some students know of the need, and this avenue eventually provided several caregivers: Allison, Lindsey, and Lynsi. Mom and Dad's next-door neighbor Janice began to help, and my friend Christie put us in contact with Annita, who eventually became a full-time caregiver.

I spent one morning a week helping with Mom's care, as well as additional times occasionally filling in for caregivers. We settled into Wednesday mornings being my morning, and I soon established a routine. After dropping the kids off at school, I drove through Starbucks to pick up coffees for Mom, Dad, Annita, and myself. Upon arriving at their house, I would join Annita in the morning routine. Annita's presence brought a joy and light that was so needed in our mornings. She loves people, and she radiates the love of Jesus. She was so gentle and attentive in her care of Mom, and she went to great lengths to make sure Mom felt beautiful, from helping her select her jewelry for the day to the attention to detail in applying Mom's makeup.

Our kids had to take on some responsibility for Mom's care as well. Because someone always had to be in the room with Mom, sometimes we asked the kids to sit with her for a few moments while we took care of other responsibilities around the house. While it was sweet to see my children caring for Mom, it also grieved me that this was the only way they remembered her. None of them had any recollection of Mom before her injury.

There was a time that Emily was asked to sit with Mom, and she had quite the scare. She heard Mom trying to talk, a very faint whisper. Emily turned to look at her, and to her shock, she saw that the ventilator tubing had popped off her trach. Emily was terrified but was able to reattach it. Thankfully, she knew what to do since no one else was in the room to help.

Chapter 17

Monsters Named Parkinson's and Dementia

The summer of 2013, Will's mom planned a long weekend for the Mayfields to all be together at Callaway Gardens in Georgia. We had a wonderful time together, staying in cabins on the property and exploring all the amenities. The cousins had a great time swimming and playing in the lake. Grandmother and Pop were rose gardeners, so it was great to walk around the gardens with them. We played games and ate meals together. The kids rode scooters. It was a really sweet time. We missed Jenny and Alex and their boys, though, as they were unable to come.

Toward the end of the summer, Will's parents came for a visit. We took them to hike with us at Burgess Falls, about an hour and a half's drive from Nashville. It was the first time we noticed Parkinson's beginning to take a toll on Dad, as he seemed to be declining physically. As our family descended the stairs to the falls, Mom and Dad turned around to walk back to the parking lot. We also noticed the physical changes at mealtimes. Dad very slowly and tediously fixed his plate each time. In spite of these changes, as far as we could tell, his mental status was still good.

In the fall of that year, it became apparent that we would need to look for a new church home for various reasons. As we began to visit churches, now with my mom and dad along with us, God led us to Christ Presbyterian Church. At the same time, we knew we needed to make a school change for all four children. We spent the fall and winter applying for admission to the academy at our new church.

Building a sense of community in a new church, especially a large one, wasn't easy. Mom's condition made it a challenge as well. We sat at the back of the church so that one of us could take her out if she had issues that had to be attended to during the service, and also to try to minimize distractions for others. She was a rather large presence, with her wheelchair, ventilator, and tubes. It can be intimidating to know how to approach people with such obvious disabilities, and to know how to interact with them. I certainly struggled with that before Mom's injury.

Even though it took some time, we found Christ Presbyterian to be a very welcoming place. Given Mom's condition, she often had to wait for others to reach out to her. Gigi Sanders, who directs the special needs ministry at our church, asked Mom to be her prayer partner for the ministry. This began a sweet friendship. They spent time together praying for the special needs ministry and for the families affected by disability.

In December, we went to Mississippi to celebrate Christmas with Will's parents, along with Jenny, Alex, and their boys. It was during this visit that I first noticed signs of dementia in Will's dad. Mom had prepared lunch and began to serve plates for everyone in the kitchen to carry into the dining room. She handed Dad his plate, and he stood there and looked up and smiled at me across the counter. Then Mom gently said, "Bill, what are you doing?" He looked at his plate and then up at me. He smiled again and said, "It's just that I've never done this before." Then we directed him to the dining room where everyone else was seated. Will had not witnessed this interaction, so I shared it with him later that evening.

As we always did when we were together, we took pictures. Sunday morning before church, I got our four kids together so I could snap a picture of them with their grandparents. As I held the camera up to my eye, I noticed that Dad was looking all around, seeming confused. Mom pointed to me and said, "Bill, now we're going to take a picture. Look there at the camera."

One day in late January of 2014, we received a short and rather abrupt email from Will's mother. It stated that Dad had closed the office at the end of the workday that day, saying he was never going back. Following the email, conversations she had with Will and his brothers were very general and rather vague in nature. She just said it was clearly time to retire and that they would be taking the steps to close his medical practice.

They came to Nashville to visit us in early February. Dad seemed a little more stooped than he had been and was moving rather slowly. He and Will ran an errand together, and they had a long conversation about his retiring, as well as a detailed and lucid conversation about finances. Will said he seemed sharp and was not too concerned about his mental status. Emily made a birthday cake for Will, and we celebrated his birthday with them. As we did almost every time we were together, Mom played piano duets and sang with Emily, and she accompanied Luke as he played violin. We also went to my parents' house for dinner. Caleb played Uno with his grandfathers. He had to explain it to Pop and give him a lot of help. On Sunday, we went to our new church together. It was a good visit.

A couple of weeks later, we received the news that the kids had all been accepted to Christ Presbyterian Academy for the coming school year. Our parents had all been praying with us about our school decision as they knew our current school had been a struggle in recent years. It was a joy to be able to share our news with them, and they were so happy for our family.

Around this time, dear Liz had major back surgery. She had struggled with back problems for so long, and she could no longer put off dealing with them. After the surgery, she moved home to Atlanta to recover. Again, God provided what we needed as far as caregiving for Mom, but oh how we missed Liz. It would be several months before she would be able to return to live with and work for Mom and Dad.

In March, Will's mom asked me to bring the children to visit them over spring break. Will was scheduled to be on call and would be unable to go with us, so I decided not to go without him. She also left me a voice mail saying they would just love to have a visit from us over spring break. These sweet, recorded words of hers would later haunt me for some time to come.

Chapter 18

Groping around in the Darkness for Hope

May 2014

Just thirty-six hours after receiving the news that Will's mother had been shot and killed, the kids and I began the drive to Jackson to join Will. We waited a day because he and his brothers needed some time there to hire an attorney for Dad and to plan the funeral for Mom. My thoughts were consumed with Will and how he was holding up. I felt lost as to how to love and care for him. When I stopped for gas, I texted our pastors Todd and David. I told them that I just could not think straight and that I needed them to give me Scriptures to read to Will. They both immediately texted back many references for verses to share with him. I did not really want to read the Bible at this point, but I knew that if there was any hope to be found in this darkness, that would be the only place we would find it.

God sustained me through that long seven-hour drive with phone calls from precious friends and family. I was on the phone for the entire drive. Friends listened to me sob as I told the story, and their voices on the other end were my lifeline to the outside world. No one gave me Bible platitudes or said this would all work for our good. I think that I would have screamed if they had. They were simply present, said they loved us and were praying, and that they agreed that this was awful.

When we arrived in Jackson, we first went to the Shaw's house, where Will, Nick, and Alex had spent the night. They had also had dinner the previous night with Boyd and Sybil Shaw and Richard and Virginia Warren, who were close friends of Will's parents.

Will and his brothers had been working tirelessly to get information about Dad, but their efforts were fruitless. Earlier in the day, they had met with and hired an attorney. Dad was transferred to a different jail.

Jenny and the boys and Tanya and her girls were all there now as well. The Shaws and others provided food for us, and we all changed clothes to go to the funeral home for the private family visitation. Mom's sisters, Frances and Amelia, and extended family were in the parking lot when we arrived.

We went inside as a family. It was still all so unbelievable. One of our children refused to go into the room and see Grandmother in the open casket, but the rest of us did. As awful as it is, this is something I believe is so important, to see the earthly home of the person you love empty and void of life. Will said it was helpful to him; it was so clear that his mom was gone from that body.

On Wednesday night, when we received the news of this tragedy, Mom's sisters Amelia and Frances were already on a train that had departed earlier that evening from Spartanburg, South Carolina, where they lived, headed to Jackson, Mississippi. They had made plans for a long weekend with Mom and Dad in Jackson, and they were also planning to go to Natchez together.

Mom had been continuing to live life with Dad, planning times like this with family. Mom and Dad also had plans for a cruise several months later, and we found her notes about that on the kitchen counter.

The visitation behind us, our family headed to stay with friends. John Biggs was in Will's medical school class; they had been very close friends. John and Jennifer had been in the singles group with us at First Presbyterian, and Mom and Dad had been John's patients.

Jennifer had kindly invited us to stay with them, and we took them up on their offer.

In all the chaos of the tragedy, they provided a little haven for our family. Their three kids were so kind and welcoming to our children, and John and Jennifer provided a quiet presence with their company as they listened and shared love and empathy with us. They fed us and made sure we were all comfortable.

Will and I finally crawled into bed once the kids were settled for the night. I did not know what to do, so I pulled out my Bible and the Scripture references David and Todd had sent me earlier in the day. I started reading aloud to Will. Thankfully, Romans 8:28 was absent from the list; if it had been present, I probably would have slammed my Bible shut. I know it is true that God works all things together for the good of those who are his, but there is a time to hear that, and it was not then. Instead, the references were for the promises of God that were comforting in that moment, and they were gentle. We were hungry to be reminded that what we believed was true.

*****

After a restless night of sporadic sleep, we awoke to Saturday, the day of Mom's funeral. Will's brothers and their families came off and on to spend time at the Biggs' house. Tanya and I went to Mom and Dad's house for the first time. I pulled up into the driveway, and that was when I saw them and completely fell apart. The roses. Mom and Dad's beloved roses. There was no one left in this house to take care of them. Mom was dead, and Dad was in jail.

I stood there staring at the roses and weeping, hugging Tanya. I think we must have gone inside the house at that point, but I don't remember.

Back at the Biggs' house, we all got dressed and prepared for the funeral. We made our way to the church, and all the extended family got into place for the receiving line two hours before the funeral. The grief was overwhelming, but so many came to help bear the burden: so many family friends and members of their church; Gracie and Linda, who had worked with Dad his entire medical career; dear friends from Nashville, the Skinners, as well as Will's dear friend William Taylor; a stream of Will's friends from Vanderbilt: Aaron, Chris, and others; Will's close high school friend, Robert. The line went on and on.

The visitation over, our entire family followed Mom's casket into the sanctuary, every pew full. Mom's oldest sister, Helen, pushed in a wheelchair by her daughters Priscilla and Mary, was crying and trying to reach out and touch the casket.

Often in church communities, funerals are renamed "celebrations of life." This has always irritated me, but now I was especially angered by it. I have wondered if it is an attempt to console those who have suffered a loss. Or is it a ploy to just ignore the grief because it makes us uncomfortable? Would we rather just gather in a church to help mourners celebrate a life instead of being present with them in their grief?

While we knew that Mom was in paradise, safe in the arms of Jesus, this did not feel like a party. Mom was sixty-seven years old and in perfect health, and her life had ended suddenly and violently in a way that made no sense. Dad was in jail, and we were all in shock. This was a time to grieve. This felt like death. It was sickening.

Pastor Steve Burton shared the hope that we have in Christ, but he also said that this was something all of us, the family and the church and the Jackson community, would have to sit in for a while. And he encouraged us to grieve and hope, grieve and hope, simultaneously.

Will and his brothers had planned the service, including some of Mom's favorites. We sang "It Is Well with My Soul" (Horatio Spafford, 1873) and "Crown Him with Many Crowns" (Matthew Bridges, 1851). I sang the words to "It Is Well" with great difficulty, not quite sure I believed what I was saying. We also answered together those comforting words to the first question from the Heidelberg Catechism, "What is your only comfort in life and death?" The answer is, "That I, with body and soul, both in life and death, am not my own, but belong unto my faithful savior Jesus Christ; who with His precious blood has fully satisfied for all my sins, and delivered me from all the power of the devil; and so preserves me that without the will of my heavenly Father not a hair can fall from my head; yea, that all things must be subservient to my salvation, wherefore by His Holy Spirit He also assures me of eternal life, and make me heartily willing and ready, henceforth, to live unto Him."

Several Scriptures were read. First Corinthians 15:50–56 is one of my favorites. Many years earlier, it was read at my grandfather's military burial, followed by the twenty-one-gun salute. He had received a Purple Heart following World War II, and the setting of hearing it at his burial was powerful.

> Behold! I tell you a mystery. We shall not all sleep, but we shall all be changed. In a moment, in the twinkling of an eye, at the last trumpet. For the trumpet will sound, and the dead will be raised imperishable, and we shall be changed. For this perishable body must put on the imperishable, and this mortal body must put on immortality. When the perishable puts on the imperishable, and the mortal puts on immortality, then shall come to pass the saying that is written: "Death is swallowed up in victory. O death, where is your victory? O death, where is your sting?" (1 Corinthians 15:51–55 ESV)

Will and I had these words memorized because we had sung them years earlier when we sang Brahms's "Requiem" with the First Presbyterian choir in Jackson.

Even though I do not recall hearing it that day, the postlude for Mom's service was "Finale from Symphony No. 5" by Charles-Marie Widor, more commonly known as Widor's "Toccata." This was appropriate as it was one of Mom's favorites. When we worshiped with them at Covenant when we were in town, if the organist played the Widor, Mom and Dad would often take the grandchildren and the rest of us up to the choir loft to watch the organist play it. It is such a joyful but very dramatic piece, and is best enjoyed by watching the organist perform it.

We went downstairs in the church, where precious church members fed us. Exhausted, we went back to collapse at the Biggs' house. Some family and close friends joined us. They just sat with us, visited, and loved us. Robert Fulcher, Will's close high school friend, had flown in from Pennsylvania to be with Will, and they spent hours together on the front porch.

As the Skinner family said their goodbyes to drive back home to Nashville, they offered to drive Will's car home so that our family could all ride home in one car. Not able to think clearly about our needs, it was something we had not even thought about. Instead of just asking if there was anything they could do, they just offered to do that one thing that day.

At some point during the weekend, we did all go to Mom and Dad's house. I remember seeing cleaning supplies and buckets in the entryway. We later found out that Pastor Steve had cleaned up the scene of the shooting. He said that he could not stand the thought of any of the family walking in on that scene. Pastors truly are the first responders for our souls, and our family is grateful for the many pastors in our lives who have been just that for us.

Chapter 19

When Your Own Family Is the One on the News

Will and his brothers had hired a wonderful attorney for Dad, but in spite of her best efforts, no one had been allowed to see Dad except for her. She said that he had spent the first night in a holding cell with fourteen other prisoners. While I know that jail is not a place where you can expect to receive excellent care, this jail had a poor reputation in regard to care of its inmates. One of Will's attorney friends called this jail a "hellhole."

Of course, the media was having a heyday with this. It was all over the news; newspapers, prime-time news, the Internet. Most stories said that it was the result of a domestic dispute, that men had been calling the house and that Dad was jealous. Some reported that it appeared an argument had taken place between them before the shooting.

It was very painful to read these words written by people who did not know our family and had no idea what had caused Dad to do this. Things are not always what they seem, even in a situation or event that seems obvious or straightforward. When we observe people or read about events, we often have no idea of a person's or a family's history or of the events that led up to it. It made me realize how I am so often guilty of judging and assuming that I know what happened to cause someone to do something, whether it is a news story or in my daily interactions with those around me. There is always a family and a story behind the headlines, and this time, it was ours.

There was one article that had a comment thread following the news story. All those who commented chose to remain anonymous. Some of the comments people posted in response to the article were hurtful, while others helped to shed some light on Dad's decline.

Included were some kind posts from family friends, stating that this was not at all Dad's character and had to have been a result of medication side effects. People who were obviously friends of theirs wrote about the dedicated caregiver Mom was for Dad. Then there were those who were curious, wanting to speculate about what medications he was on and why he would have had access to a gun. Some on the comment thread speculated that it was a result of medication levels going unattended.

There were a couple of comments that were critical of the family, saying that two of his three sons were doctors and therefore should have known how ill he was. Others criticized Mom and questioned her care of Dad. One of the worst comments was someone saying that this crime was a result of "affluenza," how affluent people can be violent, and that people spend time justifying their crimes. These words, written by people who likely did not know our family personally, were so very painful to read.

Probably the comment that shed the most light on the situation for us was from an anonymous patient of Dad's, stating, "My spouse and I are both physicians and were his patients, and raised the issue with the state medical board as to whether he was fit to practice after, first, a disturbing visit, then an alarming visit early this year. He closed his office soon after that. He does not belong in prison, and he may not even be able to assist in his own defense. I suspect if he stops his meds and his mind clears, he will be tormented until he dies once he realizes what he did" (Jackson Jambalaya, Thursday, May 1, 2014). This information was so helpful in making sense of Dad's sudden retirement earlier in the year. Either he was told he would be reported to the medical board and decided to close the doors to his practice, or the medical board shut him down.

Frances's husband, Tommy, called news stations, pleading with them, explaining that Dad was very sick with Parkinson's and needed medical care. Soon a couple of news sources reported this part of the story.

Dad's attorney said that the system still would not allow Will and his brothers to see their dad, so Sunday morning, defeated and overwhelmed with grief, we left Jackson to drive home to Nashville. Halfway into our seven-hour drive home, Will received a call from Nick. Dad had just been found down and unresponsive in his jail cell and was being transported to a local hospital. I continued to drive while Will tried to find out if they would now be allowed to see him. The answer was still no.

I felt so helpless, full of despair, and mad at God as I watched my anguished husband. And I was so angry at the system. There was just nothing we could do to help Dad.

Back home in Tennessee, we awaited news of Dad's condition. But there were no answers yet. We eventually got word that he was in renal failure.

Dad was evaluated by a prison-appointed neurologist, and we received the transcript of the evaluation. The doctor was doubtful about Dad's mental decline, saying things like, "Come on, Dr. Mayfield, you know what you did." He also said that Dad's body language told him he was faking. And to make matters worse, John Biggs, who was his primary care physician, was not allowed to see and treat him. He was handcuffed to his bed, and there was a guard at his door.

*****

Finally, a week after this horrific event, through the fierce efforts of Dad's attorney, he was transferred to St. Dominic's Hospital, where he was admitted to the neuro psych unit. Years earlier, Dad had been chief of staff here, and now he was a patient. John was now allowed to evaluate Dad and care for him. We were all very thankful for this move.

Upon examination, Dad's sides were terribly bruised, and it was confirmed he was in renal failure. While we do not have much evidence that Dad was assaulted or neglected during those few days in jail, it is not unreasonable to assume that something happened to him. The day and night of the shooting, he had been physically strong enough to probably do some yard work. He went to a concert at church with Mom, and he was able to hold, aim, and pull the trigger of a shotgun. Just three days later, he was down, unresponsive, and in renal failure. We are pretty sure he didn't receive any medical care, even though the arresting officer noted that he was possibly suffering from schizophrenia and Parkinson's.

Dad was also showing signs of rapid, significant mental decline. The blessing in this was that he did not seem to have any awareness of what he had done. He was somewhat stable physically after beginning dialysis for the kidney failure, but he was unable to eat without assistance and was unable to move his legs or walk.

A few days after being transferred, a week and a half after Mom died, Will and his brothers were finally allowed to see their dad. They spent a weekend together in Jackson, visiting Dad and checking on the house.

Will said Dad went in and out of lucid conversation during their time together. He never mentioned or asked about Mom or any other family members. At one point, he asked them if they had heard about the explosion, and he started sobbing.

In the middle of these unbelievable circumstances, God had given me something to be thankful for. I was grateful that the Lord had prompted me to call Mom on that Monday night, forty-eight hours before the shooting. Had it not been for that conversation, I would not have known about the paranoia and hallucinations Dad had been experiencing. Other family members had had some similar conversations with her during the week leading up to her death. These conversations in those last few days gave us the hope and assurance that Dad did not intend to harm the wife he loved so dearly.

Although somewhat short on details, the police report also provided some helpful information. It said that Dad "stated his name and that he called police because he shot a lady impersonating his wife." The officer also wrote, "It was discovered suspect was possibly suffering from schizophrenia along with Parkinson's disease. A neighbor stated suspect had seemed off the last couple of weeks and that suspect was found hiding in the bushes a few days ago."

Then there were the parts of the report that were truly painful to read. The officer arrived to find Dad standing on the front porch of their house. "Officer ordered him at gunpoint to show his hands; he did as instructed… Officer noticed a double-barrel shotgun lying on a table just behind him." This porch Dad was standing on was the one where we had taken family pictures together. It was where we rocked and visited on warm summer nights while watching the children play in the front yard, where Dad had held the tiny hands of his toddler grandchildren as they practiced going up and down those steps.

Also included in the report were more words I never thought I would read about my dear mother-in-law. "A white female was found lying on her back in the downstairs master bedroom with an injury to her lower right abdomen. Dispatch had already advised AMR was in route. It was discovered through the female's identification that she was in fact the suspect's wife."

Chapter 20

Dad Becomes a Free Man

At home, we were struggling through our normal daily routines while waiting for updates on Dad's health, as well as what would happen as far as the charges against him. The state was beginning to prepare a murder trial; this was unbelievable.

Will wanted to see his dad again, and we felt like it was important for all of us to go. So, Memorial Day weekend, we packed the van and headed to Jackson to visit Dad.

My prayer leading up to this visit was that the kids would hear Pop say things that made it obvious to them that he was not himself. Instead, we walked into his hospital room, and he was asleep. He never woke up during our visit. I had brought Sally Lloyd-Jones's book *Thoughts to Make Your Heart Sing* along with us. This book, as well as *The Jesus Storybook Bible*, had been so meaningful to our family in recent years. It had been meaningful to me, personally, because during these years of tragedy, I needed a childlike faith again.

I had bookmarked several pages for us to read to Dad. Perhaps my favorite reading we read to him that day is titled "Resting and Relying." It includes a beautiful illustration of a sleeping toddler resting his head on his daddy's shoulder. In it Sally says, "Faith is leaning your whole weight on God. Resting your head on his shoulder" (pp. 76–77). I read to Dad a bit and then asked the kids if they would like to read to Pop as well. William offered to read aloud, and he ministered to us all as he so thoughtfully and compassionately stood next to Pop's bedside reading such comforting words that we all needed to hear. The other three kids were very nervous to be there and didn't seem to want to get too close to Pop.

I kissed Dad on the forehead and said goodbye, and I took the kids to play at the park across the street so that Will could have some time alone with his dad.

Luke later told me that he was afraid to be in the room with a man who had killed his own wife. He said he was afraid that Pop might kill him too. I realized in that moment that in getting ready for this visit, I had not thought to prepare the children and address their fears and feelings.

Emily had been so angry with Pop from the moment she heard the news, even though we explained that Pop had not intended to kill Grandmother. I soon realized that it was important to let her grieve how she needed to grieve, even if that meant not interfering in her anger toward Pop.

Dad's nurse said that he had been mostly asleep and not eating for the past twenty-four hours. He had an NG tube for feedings. He had been pulling at it, so he had been restrained. When the nurse talked to us about him, she called him a name other than Bill (I believe it was the name of a fish). Because of the nature of the case, Dad was an anonymous patient. This was upsetting to hear. It really bothered Will, and the kids were confused. Will gently said to the nurse, "Bill. His name is Bill."

She told us that he was scheduled to have a procedure to have a PEG tube placed the next week. Given Dad's continued decline, Will discussed this with his brothers. Because Dad's body seemed to be naturally shutting down, they did not want to prolong his suffering. Also, according to Dad's living will, he did not want his life artificially prolonged. So they made the decision to cancel the procedure. NG feedings and dialysis were also stopped.

End-of-life care is a painfully sensitive issue that is not to be taken lightly. It involves decisions that will have lasting ramifications, whether the person lives or dies. With a bleak and terminal diagnosis, should a family member receive a PEG tube for long-term nutrition, eventually be put on a ventilator, or have other procedures done to indefinitely and artificially prolong life? Does he have a living will stating his wishes? Each situation is unique. While we may be tempted to judge others for decisions in these situations, we need to remember that what they need is compassion in their suffering and grief.

Will and his brothers made this decision with prayer, trusting that this was the best decision for Dad. All three of them were in agreement about this, which was a huge blessing. Had they been divided, the decision would have been even more painful.

Because Dad was a believer and his hope was in Jesus, we knew where he would be going after he drew his last breath. He would immediately be in heaven, in the presence of the Lord.

I want to be sensitive here because I realize that there are those of you who have faced these decisions for those whose faith was not in Jesus. This is not something we have dealt with, and I cannot begin to imagine the pain and grief involved.

A few days after our visit with Dad, he entered hospice care. Will received daily reports on his condition. The news was that he was sleeping peacefully all day and night.

*****

Late in the afternoon of June 6, after a week in hospice and just five weeks after Mom's death, Will received the phone call that we had been waiting for. Dad had died peacefully in his sleep at the age of sixty-eight.

Although we did not want to lose Dad, we were so thankful that the Lord in his great mercy decided to take him home. The system that had failed Dad had no power over him now. Instead of being surrounded by prison bars, he was wrapped in the arms of Jesus surrounded by the "great cloud of witnesses" mentioned in the book of Hebrews. Instead of going through a trial in a courtroom and being found guilty of murder, he was ushered into the throne room of heaven and found to be innocent because of what Jesus accomplished on his behalf. Dad was home, he was well, and he was free. Not only that, but we are promised that heaven is a place without tears, sorrow, and guilt over sin. At the sight of his wife, Dad did not experience anguish and sorrow. It was a perfect, joyful reunion. Amazing!

Again, God gave us the ministry of presence, as one of our pastors, Ken Leggett, came to our house that evening to sit with Will. He just sat and listened. When he did speak, it was to agree with Will that what had happened to Dad Mayfield and the losses Will had experienced were awful.

While they sat, I went upstairs to tuck the children in. I once again picked up *The Jesus Storybook Bible* and read aloud to them while choking back tears. In one particular story, Sally Lloyd-Jones writes about the account in Mark 4 and Matthew 8, when Jesus and his disciples are on a boat in a terrible storm, and Jesus is asleep! The following are my favorite words from "The Captain of the Storm."

> Jesus stood up and spoke to the storm. "Hush!" he said. That's all. And the strangest thing happened… The wind and the waves recognized Jesus' voice. (They had heard it before, of course—it was the same voice that made them, in the very beginning.) They listened to Jesus and they did what he said. Immediately the wind stopped… Then Jesus turned to his wind-torn friends. "Why were you scared?" he asked. "Did you forget who I Am? Did you believe your fears, instead of me?" (*The Jesus Storybook Bible*, Sally Lloyd-Jones, 2007)

As I was so controlled by fear and grief, these words ministered to me as a reminder that I belong to the great I Am.

*****

Will and his brothers began to make arrangements, and they decided to wait a week to have the service.

For months, Mom had been planning a family summer vacation at the beach. A dear, kind friend of theirs had offered their beach house for our whole family to use. Mom had been so excited about it. After Mom and Dad died, their friends again extended the offer of their house. We decided it would be good for our three families to have some time away together after Dad's funeral.

Once again, our families met in Jackson for a funeral. The morning of June 14, our families had a small service to place Mom's and Dad's ashes together in the church's columbarium. Mom had had a significant role in planning this very columbarium years earlier. She had helped design this beautiful space where we now placed her remains, along with Dad's.

Again, we entered a sanctuary full of friends and family joining us to say goodbye to Dad. And again, dear friends and church members fed us and loved us well.

Our families spent some time together going through things at the house. We did some cleaning out and allowed the children to choose some things that were important to them. It was so strange being in the house without Mom and Dad. I expected to hear Mom's heels on the brick floor any minute, but only silence came.

With Mom's death being so sudden, we were left without the gift of her recorded words about suffering that we had been given with my mom. But Mom Mayfield was a gifted artist. When we went into the house soon after the shooting, her most recent pastel was on the easel, mostly finished. She had not even signed it yet, but we know from talking to her that she had worked on it with her art teacher the day before she died.

The painting was of a beautiful, peaceful countryside scene. Her teacher touched up a couple of small spots that Mom had not yet finished. We took it and had giclées made so that each of our three families would have one. They now adorn the walls of our houses, joining other works of hers.

Following this time together in Jackson, our three families headed for the beach. We spent a couple of nights there together. It was a bittersweet time, enjoying watching the kids play together on the beach, but missing Mom and Dad, who were supposed to be here with us.

Chapter 21

Pieces of the Puzzle and Grieving Together

After Mom and Dad Mayfield died, Will and his brothers were able to sit down and talk with Dad's physicians. Even though there were still so many unanswered questions, it was somewhat helpful to hear from them. They said that they saw a sharp, sudden decline in Dad's condition in the six weeks leading up to the shooting. For the most part, he was lucid during the day, and the severe hallucinations and paranoia came at night. One physician said that he was planning to talk to Mom soon about possibly putting Dad in a nursing home.

They also never had a definitive diagnosis for Dad as they had been somewhat baffled by his illness over the last few years. It was always called a "Parkinson's-like condition." While Dad was dying, Will called several research hospitals, hoping that one of them might be able to do a postmortem brain biopsy so that we might have a definite diagnosis, but none of them were willing to do so. We would have to learn to live with a lack of answers about Dad's condition and also about what exactly had happened the night of the shooting.

With Dad's death and funeral behind us, Will and his brothers continued to work through their parents' estate business. Tanya worked hard to create a document with pictures and descriptions of furniture and other items in the house. Tanya knew that Mom had a document somewhere on her computer that included pictures and brief histories of many of the antique furniture pieces and accessories in their home. She was finally able to locate it. It was so sweet to read Mom's words about special pieces that each of our families were able to take into their homes.

So we all began the process of sorting through and dividing their earthly possessions. I am grateful for how peaceful this process was for our families. Our families all returned to Jackson at different times to sort through things and take them home.

To me, the hardest things to claim and take with us were the things my children had made for their grandparents, as well as the sweet notes and letters they had written to them. But I couldn't throw them away, so I took them home.

And then there was the yard. For many years, Mom and Dad had planted and cultivated a gorgeous rose garden in their backyard. Through an email, we learned that precious neighbors, including a master gardener, had banded together to care for the roses since Mom's death and Dad's arrest. This was a gift to our family to see signs of life at the house each time we returned.

Our family went back to Jackson again in early July to continue to sort through things. We wanted to be sure to find things that would be meaningful before the rest of it became a part of the estate sale. Again, the Biggs family showed us sweet hospitality, welcoming us into their home for the weekend.

*****

That summer, Emily was scheduled to spend two weeks at Camp Hollymont for her fourth summer there. We had several talks about camp and whether she wanted to spend two weeks away from family after all that had happened. Emily was our camp girl—she absolutely loved it! She did admit to being a little nervous, but in the end, she decided that she still really wanted to go.

I wanted to take Will away for a few days while Emily was at camp. My parents and Mom's caregivers graciously agreed to take care of the boys. So I surprised him by booking a few nights in Estes Park, Colorado, where we had honeymooned seventeen years earlier.

In July, we packed Emily for camp, and the kids and I made the drive to Asheville to spend the night before dropping her off at camp the next morning. We all had a good night's sleep at the hotel, but at breakfast the next morning, I noticed that Emily was unusually quiet. After eating, we went back to the room to pack up. Before leaving the hotel room, I sat down with the kids to pray. Emily began to sob… and sob. I hugged her and held her. But it continued to escalate. She felt as though she could not breathe, and she ran to the bathroom, where she threw up several times. I had never actually witnessed a panic attack before, but after about half an hour, I realized that this was what was happening to her.

I called Will back home because I knew it would help her to hear his voice and talk through it with him. I had communicated with camp earlier in the summer about our family circumstances, but I called the office to let them know what was going on with her that morning. They were so gracious and said that she had been through a lot in the past few months and that they would completely understand if she did not come. They also said they would apply what we had paid for camp to next summer's fees.

After talking to Will, we told her the decision about camp needed to be hers. She decided to go home with us. She felt terrible that we had driven all the way there only for her to be going home. I was sad for her, and it grieved my heart to see her struggling. I was worried that she would regret her decision, but she never did. Several times over the summer, she would say, "Mom, it was the right decision, and I don't regret it. I needed to be with my family this summer."

Will and I had a wonderful time together in Colorado. We hiked many miles over those three days. Some of the hikes were very challenging, and it was good to conquer them together. Some miles were spent talking and processing together, but we hiked many of them in silence. Hiking in the cool mountain air and taking in breathtaking views was therapeutic.

We also spent time reading, talking, and just sitting in silence on the porch of our little cabin at McGregor Mountain Lodge. Our conversations here seventeen years earlier had been so different, so full of hope for the future, and without much understanding and experience of loss and suffering. Strangely, though, because of what we had experienced, there was a richness in our time together.

Our reading material wasn't exactly what we would have ever considered to be enjoyable vacation reading. We began to read *Walking with God through Pain and Suffering* by Tim Keller. One of Tim's most profound statements in the book is this: "God gives us what we would have asked for if we knew everything that He knows." While my mind knows that God does all things for our good and his glory, that is a tough statement for my heart to wrestle with.

While we were gone, the kids enjoyed their time with Mom, Dad, and the caregivers. They also got to spend a day helping with Very Special Bible School at our church. Our church has a beautiful ministry to those with special needs and their families; VSBS is just one event of that ministry. We were so thankful the kids got to experience that. It became the starting point of our family's involvement in the ministry.

In early August, Will and his brothers went back to Jackson for one last weekend there together. They stayed in the house this time, and they spent more time going through things and dividing furniture and other items. Will had the realization that up until this point, the house still looked pretty much the same as it did when Mom and Dad were still living. He knew that if he ever returned again, it wouldn't be the same, and it wouldn't be their house anymore.

Chapter 22

Valleys, Victories, and Everything in Between

In the fall, all four of our kids began the new school year at Christ Presbyterian Academy. They did remarkably well adjusting to their new school, considering all they had been through the past few months. Will was quiet and reflective and continued to work faithfully to take care of his patients and to provide for our family.

I continued to do the things necessary to run our household and to help with my mom, but I was struggling. I cried a lot and felt physically exhausted, and I was unable to motivate myself to meet new people and get very involved at our new school. I mostly spoke to people I already knew. It was just too hard to make conversation with people who were unaware of what had happened in our family.

Soon after the tragedy, I did write a social media post about what had happened. I continued to add pictures because it seemed to be meaningful to family and friends. I think the pictures provided a good visual reminder of who Mom and Dad Mayfield really were. So many people left encouraging comments and words of comfort.

One of the most profound comments was from our friend Ingrid Curry. After she said how sorry she was about what had happened, she said something like this: "Julie, our heavenly Father takes us all home in different ways." This statement has played over in my mind so many times since then. It was a reminder to me that death is the avenue to eternal life. In order for there to be a resurrection, there has to be a death. Death is painful and feels very wrong. People die young and old, and in many different ways. This was the way God took Will's parents home, and it was another reminder that we do not have to understand. We are to trust God and believe him.

I knew that everyone in our family was grieving, but I felt like something else was wrong with me. Why were they able to concentrate on work and school, while I was unable to focus on the simplest tasks? Finishing a load of laundry or going to the grocery store were draining. These types of chores completely wiped me out.

Will and I discovered that we grieve very differently. I needed to talk about it…a lot. And he is a great listener and was very patient with me. Will is quiet, but he found that the shower and the woods were great places to cry and yell.

I also noticed that he would frequently retreat when around a lot of people. Will and I are both introverts, so this is fairly normal behavior for us anyway. However, I began to notice that he would withdraw, leaving gatherings, Sunday school sometimes, more than usual. I was not too alarmed by this because I knew he just needed the quiet more than usual now.

When pastors and friends called and emailed to check on Will, he repeatedly asked one thing: "Please pray that I will run to God and not away from him." And even though he was grieving deeply, Will did that. He continued to pray and cry out to God, and he stayed in the Bible. These were the very things I was struggling with and unable to do most days. But as I watched Will continue to walk with God and wrestle with him over his parents' deaths, it gave me a glimmer of hope that God hadn't forgotten us.

In mid-September, an estate sale was finally held at Mom and Dad's house in Jackson, the last step in getting the house ready to go on the market. None of the family wanted to be there, as it would have been too painful to watch the house slowly grow empty of its contents.

After the mistreatment and death of their dad, Will and his brothers were encouraged by some to bring action against the state. While they did desire justice for their dad, to see reform in the

Mississippi justice system, and for those responsible for the mistreatment of their dad to be held accountable, they believed it would be a costly, uphill battle that was unlikely to bring about any change. They were also devastated and grieving hard, and a long battle would have added to the grief. So they ultimately decided not to do so. But they did desire to have Dad's record cleared. On September 16, Dad's attorney finally received notice that the case of *State vs. Dr. William Mayfield, Jr.* had reached the assistant DA's office back in July.

In a letter from the assistant district attorney's office, it is stated that, "Prior to deliberation the Grand Jury received all of the evidence in the case which included extensive testimony regarding Dr. William Mayfield, Jr.'s mental status at the time of the shooting. After deliberation, the Grand Jury returned a 'No Bill' finding specifically that Dr. William Mayfield, Jr. lacked the requisite mental capacity to commit a crime on the night his wife was shot."

Mom's death certificate does say that the cause of death was "shotgun wound to the abdomen," and "homicide" is listed as the type of death. While those words are difficult to read, we know that ultimately it was Dad's terrible disease that pulled the trigger, not him.

There were many places in Scripture that were an encouragement to Will, but a couple really gave him hope. And they are not the typical verses we think of during trials. For Will, 2 Timothy 4:14 was a great comfort to him: "Alexander the coppersmith did me great harm; the Lord will repay him according to his deeds." This was particularly comforting to Will, knowing that God had seen what had happened to Dad in jail; God had seen those who had harmed him. It allowed Will to begin the journey of forgiving those who had harmed his dad, even though they would likely remain anonymous to him. The names and faces of fellow inmates, wardens, and others who possibly harmed Bill Mayfield might always remain a mystery to the family. Even so, we are called to forgive. This is hard and is only possible when we acknowledge the depth of our own sin.

And then, three simple words found several places in Scripture, including Romans 4:3, Galatians 3:6, James 2:23, and others: "Abraham believed God." For Will, it was comforting that he didn't need to understand why God allows the sufferings he does. He just needed to believe and trust him. Will said that God's promises are not based on our feelings. They are based on the strength of the resurrection, and without the resurrection, there is no hope in our loss and pain. But if the resurrection is true, then God really has conquered death, and he really can fulfill those promises that we will live with him forever. Psalm 119:50 says, "This is my comfort in my affliction, that your promise gives me life" (ESV). I learned a lot from Will and from watching him both wrestle and believe.

Will and his brothers remained silent to comments made on news articles and social media. There had also been critical comments directed toward them, and they did not respond. This is a truly beautiful, remarkable characteristic in a human being. And I greatly admired Will and his brothers for looking the other way when their character was called into question.

I was having great difficulty trusting and believing God in all of this. I was angry with him and questioning him. I talked to Will a lot about this. One night, I remember saying, "I need some hope. I have hope for eternity, and I really do believe that Jesus will come back one day and make all things new. But where in the world am I supposed to find hope for now, for while we're still here?"

Will's response was, "I believe our future hope spills backwards and gives us hope in the present. I think I heard Tony Giles say that." I could see the truth in that, but it took a while for it to sink in and for me to believe it.

*****

Now that we were fairly established in our large church, Will felt it was important to be in a small group to help us cultivate a sense of community. He was asked to lead one, and I was just not on board. I did not have it in me to meet a group of new people who had no idea what we had been going through the last few months. We hosted the group in our home, and while I did my best to put on a smiling face for the group, I was surly about it toward Will.

Our group disbanded after the required six weeks, but we did end up with some sweet new friends once it was over. One evening, Will shared our recent family events with Christian Barr. Christian remembered that his family had been friends with Will's family when they all lived in Jacksonville, Florida. I found pictures of Will and Christian together when they were two to three years old. We have loved getting to know Christian and Emily and their family ever since. What a small world!

Later in the fall of 2014, my mom's overall health seemed to decline. She was just not feeling well, and it was frustrating for Dad and the caregivers to know how best to help her.

Since Mom's injury, Dad had been able to get away occasionally. As a caregiver, it was very important for him to be refreshed by stepping away from the intensity of her care. In October, he took Will, Jeff, and Todd to Cape Cod with him for three nights. The kids and I stayed at Mom and Dad's house, and I took Dad's place as the overnight caregiver.

Although it was a daunting responsibility, it gave me a great appreciation for what Dad did for her every single night. I set an alarm to wake me up at 2:00 a.m. and 6:00 a.m. During these times, I had to roll Mom into a new position in the bed, give her water, check and empty the ostomy and catheter bags, and take care of anything else she needed. There were also random times during the night when she woke me because she needed me to cough her, or because she wanted a drink of water. When we did settle down between these times, I lay wide awake, listening for her every breath.

At Bible study one day in October, our small group shared prayer requests as we did every week. When it was my turn, I fell apart. I cried as I shared the heavy weight of grief over Will's parents and how Mom was not doing well.

One of my small group leaders, Karen Anderson, sent me a simple text later that day. It said, "How can I help?" Those four words were a lifeline to me, even though it was difficult to put into words what I needed. She suggested we go for a walk, so a few days later, we did. We walked and walked on the trails at Percy Warner Park, and she listened as I talked.

Toward the end of our time that day, she said, "Friend, I will continue to walk through this with you, but I think you also need some professional help." At first, I was shocked that she said that. I had never been to counseling, and I certainly did not think I needed it; I was offended. But I listened, mainly because she said she would stick with me through this. She wasn't trying to hand me off to someone else because I was too difficult. She was not abandoning me. That was huge.

It took me a little time to come around and admit that I needed counseling. And when I did, I was so down that I lacked the mental energy to even figure out where to begin. So I just asked Karen who I should call, and she gave me Margaret's name. I was terrified to make the initial phone call, but I eventually did.

*****

It may sound simple, but admitting I needed help was a huge step in my journey to finding healing. As I pulled into the driveway for my first appointment, I was unsure I could find the courage to even go inside. But God carried me, and in spite of my great fear, I did go inside.

As part of her counseling, Margaret requires her new clients to write summaries of what led them to come to her. I sat on the sofa as she read what I had written. After a few minutes, she looked up and said, "Wow, this is a lot." We talked for a bit about the tragic events our family had been through, and also about how I was doing.

Then she stunned me by asking, "How long has the depression been going on?" I was offended and told her I was there about grief. She continued to probe, asking hard questions, and I realized she was right.

I was sinking deeper and deeper into depression with each passing day. I felt like I was in a deep, dark hole, and everyone else was walking around living life on ground level above me. I wanted so badly to get up there to see how they were functioning. I wanted to join them, but I was stuck.

As we talked further and went back in time, we realized that my first memorable bout with depression was during my freshman year of college. That was a very difficult year for me, as it is for many. I was feeling down, my sleep schedule was off, and I struggled to keep up with my schoolwork. And I was lonely. I did not have words for what was going on inside my head. Even if I had known I was depressed at the time, I would not have known who to talk to or what to do about it. I'm pretty sure there wasn't even a counselor in my town at the time.

In college, the other problem was that I knew something was wrong with me, but I did not want anyone else to know. I wanted to hide. I was involved in a campus ministry, and I have a vivid memory of the campus minister confronting me one day, asking, "Are you doing all right?" I felt cornered and said, "Oh, of course, I'm doing fine!"

And then Margaret and I discussed the depression after the deliveries of two of my babies. I am certain I had postpartum depression, but I was ashamed and didn't mention it to my doctor either time.

I also began to really struggle with depression again after Mom's car accident and injury. Since I did not address it, the depression had gotten deeper in the nine years following that event. I would not even listen when my close friend Catha suggested counseling might be helpful.

As if it was not bad enough to give my struggle the name of depression, Margaret also encouraged me to see my doctor about getting on medication, since I had been struggling for so long. She explained that this, along with counseling, would be helpful in battling the depression.

This was a lot to process after our first meeting, but before leaving her office, I made an appointment to see her again the next week.

Will and I talked about it later that evening, and he was really resistant to me taking antidepressants. So we decided to wait.

*****

Two of Mom's caregivers, Allison and Lindsey, were also student athletes at Trevecca Nazarene University. In November of 2014, the school hosted the Conquer the Challenge 5K run. Since Mom had always loved running, they decided they would enter the race together.

So on a chilly November morning, Lindsey and Allison began Mom's morning routine extra early, waking up at five forty-five to get ready for the race later that morning. Mom was nervous about the cold, so they dressed her in plenty of layers, including blankets and a hat.

Upon arriving at Trevecca, Mom was welcomed by a large group of athletes clapping and cheering for her as she came out of the van.

Mom's chair is very heavy, and Lindsey and Allison ran together, pushing Mom up and down hills along the course, occasionally helped by other athletes along the way. Mom, being the coach that she always had been, coached them along the way, telling them she wanted to finish in under thirty minutes. They did! They finished in twenty-eight minutes.

They were greeted at the finish line by athletes cheering them on. A young man ran out to help lift Mom's front wheels over a speed bump so her wheelchair could cross the finish line!

On finishing the race, Mom was asked by an interviewer, "Lynn, how did it feel to finish?" With a huge smile on her face, Mom said, "It felt great!" Mom's voice was weak and quiet, but she was so excited that she continued to try to tell the interviewer all about it!

Mom, Lindsey, and Allison's experience was videoed from the moment Mom was unloaded from the van until the interview after the race. The university submitted it as an entry in the NCAA 2015 Division II Award of Excellence, which recognizes schools for their meaningful involvement with their local communities. Trevecca Nazarene University was one of twenty-five universities selected as a finalist. We were so grateful for Mom to have this experience!

Mom had always been a fierce competitor. When Mom and I had been running partners years before, she constantly pushed me beyond what I thought I was capable of. The fastest times I ever ran were during races with her by my side. In fact, at the start of one of our 5K's, they announced that there would be a prize for the first parent/child to cross the finish line together. The entire race, she was eyeing pairs that we needed to get ahead of, and I could not believe how fast she was pushing me to run! We crossed the finish line in a time that I will never come close to again. We had done it. We had won the prize for the first parent/child team.

Chapter 23

Holidays and Depression

In November, as if we had not had enough change and stress, we decided to buy a house closer to school and church. We hired a contractor to do renovations before we moved in.

In addition, Will put his carpentry skills to use. Over the course of a few months, he built an entire wall of built-in bookshelves and cabinets in our new living room. Having a project proved to be therapeutic for him as he continued to grieve the loss of his parents.

My side of the family had our annual Thanks-Christmas, as our kids like to call it, hosted by my parents. Since Thanksgiving is the holiday we spend together, we combine our Thanksgiving and Christmas celebrations. We have Christmas morning, opening gifts around the tree, and follow that with Thanksgiving dinner. Shopping is one of the few things Mom was able to do, and she loved choosing just the right gifts for her family. With the use of her eye-gaze computer, she was able to independently shop and order gifts online. And she also loved to go shopping at the mall and Target with her caregivers.

But this particular Thanksgiving, Mom was very different. She was not feeling well; she was lethargic and depressed. In spite of all the activity around her, she spent a lot of time sleeping in her wheelchair.

Holidays are a difficult time of the year when your family is dependent upon caregivers for a family member. In Mom's case, her care was so specialized that only people trained to care for her were able to help. And the major holidays were times when the caregivers needed time off to be with their families.

When Mom and Dad were in the Atlanta area, the holidays fell to Dad and Susan and Todd. Almost every major holiday for seven years, Todd and Susan and their family were unable to travel to see his family or do other things.

I knew this but never understood the stress and sadness in it until Mom and Dad moved to Nashville. It also made me regret deeply that we had never met as a family to establish a holiday caregiving schedule so that it did not fall to my sister every time. In hindsight, I wish our extended family had sat down together early on to establish how we would support one another in our new caregiving roles. I wish we had sat down to have honest conversations about how hard it was to watch Mom suffer and to care for her, because I know for me, it really was. I want to encourage anyone in a situation like this to sit down and have these hard conversations. Communicating openly and honestly is so important.

So when it fell to me to become the holiday caregiver, it gave me great empathy for Susan's family and what they did all those years in Georgia. In all honesty, I did not just grow in empathy. Something sinful began to grow as well. I began to grow resentful toward my siblings for not being there to help during holidays.

I will just say it. Caregiving is hard. Yes, suffering is extremely difficult on the one who is enduring the suffering. But caregiving for the person with extreme needs is very demanding physically and emotionally. I believe as caregivers, we often don't want to be honest out of fear of making the patient feel like a burden.

Mom's routine was extremely monotonous and demanding. The daily meticulous, life-sustaining care would never improve her condition. Yes, it would keep her alive, but she would remain the same. This was hard. It was agonizing. Bathe, administer medications, feed, give sips of water, stretch, trach care, cough, massage head, change dressings, empty ostomy bag, empty catheter bag, dress, undress. Repeat. Multiple times a day. Every single day. Watching my mom suffer like this every day was taking a toll and was getting to be too much for me to handle.

For the whole week of Christmas, Dad cared for Mom alone all day unless I was there helping or they were with our family. Each morning, I spent several hours helping Dad with Mom's morning care and getting her up in her chair. Then, each night, I spent several hours helping him get her settled into bed for the night. It was hard as a mom not to be able to read to my children at bedtime and tuck them in. On Christmas morning, Mom was patient and stayed in bed longer than usual so that I could have Christmas morning with my family.

It was during this week that I hit rock bottom. I snapped. Will arrived home from work one evening to find me crying at the stove as I prepared dinner. From there, it escalated into a full-blown panic attack. He took me up to the bonus room to lie down. I was sobbing uncontrollably, struggling to breathe, and feeling as though an elephant were sitting on my chest. Will patiently and lovingly sat with me until it subsided.

As we talked later that night, Will said that maybe some medication would be beneficial, and that he would be okay with that. I made an appointment to see my doctor a few days later and began to take antidepressants for the first time in my life.

I will pause here, in defense of Will. His delay in considering me taking medication for depression is justified. As a physician, he sees the dangers of the side effects of certain medications. Becoming dependent on antidepressants, as well as the inability to come off them with time, are legitimate concerns. I was grateful to have both Will and my doctor to be accountable to during this process.

It was already difficult to tell friends that I was going to counseling, but for me, taking medication added another layer of shame. And it was hard to tell Mom and Dad. Since Mom's accident, she had been taking medication for anxiety and depression, but they had never been to counseling. I think the counseling part of my treatment was the hardest part for them to understand.

After the holidays, I continued to go to counseling, and after a month or so, I could begin to feel the effects of the antidepressants. I was still very down, but it helped me think a little more clearly as I began to process more through counseling. One thing Margaret encouraged me to do was to find a new right-brain activity, whether that was through music or art. However, the thought of learning something new was frightening, and I was just too exhausted.

She gave me simple but helpful strategies to implement in those moments of complete despair. For example, "Feel yourself on the chair, your feet touching the floor. Gravity is still working. God is still in control."

We talked about Dad Mayfield's time in jail, the suffering he endured, and the family's inability to do anything to help and protect him. Margaret reminded me that because Dad belonged to Jesus, he was not alone. She asked if I had ever thought about the fact that the Spirit, and possibly angels, were there in his cell ministering to him. She encouraged me to picture that every time I had a thought of him being beaten and mistreated in jail.

My meetings with Margaret continued to be productive and encouraging. And they were helpful to Will, as well. On the days I met with Margaret, later in the evening I shared with Will the things she shared with me that were helpful. In almost every meeting, Margaret continued to tell me I really needed to find something new to do with art or music. My brain needed something new and beautiful to think about. But I was just not able do it.

Chapter 24

Vacation and Anniversary Grief

In the spring of 2015, we were able to travel and spend our spring break at Disney World and Universal Studios in Orlando. It was a much-needed getaway, as we felt it was important to have this time away to just play together as a family.

We spent the first half of the week at Universal. It was wonderful to soak in the sun by the pool and play in the parks together. We all love Harry Potter, and we had a great time reliving the books through all the rides and details in Hogsmeade and Diagon Alley and, of course, on the Hogwarts Express.

The last few days were spent at Disney. Caleb was now tall enough for Rock-n-Roller Coaster, so the boys and Will and I made some great memories riding it. Coasters are not a favorite for Emily, so she was able to do some exploring on her own. Of course, we rode some of her favorites with her.

It was a good week making some new, recent, sweet memories and just having fun in magical kingdoms. Isn't it interesting that God has given us a desire for a better kingdom? I think for many, myself included, this is why we are drawn to places like Disney World. We long for happiness, for a magical place away from the cares of this world. I remember David Filson saying that in a sermon once. God has ultimately given us a longing for his kingdom, which is beyond any earthly kingdom we can imagine. No more pain, tears, sickness, or suffering. And the promise of perfect communion with Jesus.

Soon after our vacation, around the one-year anniversary of the shooting, I saw that Luke was really struggling with what I now know to be anniversary grief. I realize now that some family counseling early on might have been beneficial for all of us. But a year later, I felt like it might make some in the family more uncomfortable, so we had Luke see a counselor at DayStar Ministries for a while. It was difficult to tell if it was beneficial for him at the time; he was ten years old. But he did enjoy going, and his counselor was great.

Emily was continuing to struggle with intense anxiety, mostly when she was away overnight from our family. So we also sought counseling for her. While it was not a solution for her anxiety, it was beneficial.

By the end of May, the renovations on our new house were finally complete, and we made the move across town. For me, it was a bittersweet move. It was sad to leave our house knowing that our new one would not hold memories of visits from Will's parents. But it was sweet to have a fresh start with a house, to leave the bedroom where we received the call that Will's mom had not survived her gunshot wound. The bedroom where we tossed and turned and cried all night in the darkness.

We spent the summer unpacking and getting settled. The boys participated in camps at school, and the kids and I had the joy of volunteering with Very Special Bible School at our church. Emily spent two weeks at Camp Hollymont. Since this was the last summer she was eligible to be a camper, we were so thankful God gave her the courage to go.

*****

When fall of that year came, Mom wasn't feeling well. Her symptoms were similar to those of the year before: depression, lethargy, pain. But this time, she seemed much worse. Many quadriplegics struggle with constant pain. Mom was one of these, but the nature of the injury can make it difficult for them to identify the source of the pain.

October rolled around, and Mom no longer wanted to get up in her wheelchair. When she did, through the encouragement of care-givers, she would often moan in pain and ask to go back to bed. Getting out of bed was necessary to avoid pressure sores that had the potential to break down her skin and cause a multitude of problems.

One morning, I arrived to visit Mom. When I walked into the bedroom and saw her face, it was obvious that something was seri-ously wrong. She was sitting up in bed with a look in her wide eyes that told me she was only partially with us. She seemed to be looking *through* us. It is a look I will never forget. I talked to Dad, and we decided to take her to the emergency room.

Upon arriving at the emergency room, we were quickly taken into a room. We described what had been going on with her. Extreme pain, lethargy, not eating well, wanting to stay in bed all day. They ran some labs on her blood and urine, all of which came back fairly normal. I mentioned the ovarian cancer from ten years earlier. I asked about the possibility of ordering a scan of her abdominal area to see if the cancer had returned. This suggestion was brushed off, and so was her pain. They gave her one IV dose of morphine, in a manner that seemed as though it was to humor us. Then they sent us on our way. I was angry. And too late, I regretted not being a better advocate for her.

In defense of the physician who saw us, and because I am mar-ried to one, I know they are not God. They are human, and most do their very best to diagnose and treat patients. Ventilator-dependent quadriplegics are very challenging patients, and there are very few of them. Over the years, Mom had good physicians, but for most of them, her care was a challenge, to say the least.

So with no help and no answers, we continued to care for Mom and do whatever we could to make her comfortable, which was almost impossible. Dad and the caregivers made the decision to let her stay in bed almost all day most days, since this seemed to be where she wanted to be. On Halloween, we took the kids over to trick-or-treat at her bedside.

*****

By November, Mom was no longer able to get up in her wheelchair to go to church. When one of our pastors, David Filson, heard about this, he made an announcement in our Sunday school class that because she was sick and unable to get to worship, he and some others would be taking worship to her. He invited our Sunday school class to join us in her bedroom on Sunday afternoon.

Later that afternoon, we gathered around Mom's bed: Dad, our family, the Filson family, caregivers, and dear Liby from our Sunday school class. David brought his guitar and led us in some hymns and worship music. His dear wife, Diane, and their children, Luke and Lydia, brought communion and served it to Mom and all of us. And of course, David preached a life-giving sermon. Mom was struggling so much that she choked on the small bite of communion bread. An episode with the cough machine ensued, Lynsi using the suction to clear her airway. Once her airway was cleared and she was calm again, Mom said, "At least I got to taste it."

David said he would be back the following Sunday. Before he left, Mom requested songs for the next time, one of which was "Whom Shall I Fear? (God of Angel Armies)" by Chris Tomlin (2012). David and his family returned the following week for another bedside worship service, and he did indeed lead in the singing of "Whom Shall I Fear? (God of Angel Armies)." These times of worship together were truly a treasure.

There were other routines and activities of Mom's that ceased to happen. She stopped watching movies and television in her room. She did not want much music anymore. Her world was becoming smaller; it was defined by the four walls of their bedroom and the people who came to visit her there. Most of her nutrition was now through her feeding tube. She slept a lot during the day and moaned off and on in pain when she was awake.

Chapter 25

Thanksgiving, Followed by Death

Thanksgiving week came, and with it came my siblings and their families. This was a very different visit. Mom stayed in bed the whole time. On Wednesday, the day before Thanksgiving, I arrived to help with Mom's morning care. Annita and I rolled Mom onto her side so that Annita could wash her back. Annita felt something on Mom's back and asked me to put my hand there. Whether it was a mass or fluid, we did not know. Dad called her primary care physician and told him what was going on. He said that it sounded as though her body was shutting down and that he would put in orders for hospice care to begin after the Thanksgiving weekend. Again, this was a time that we should have fought for her, for those orders to be done immediately. I realize that looking back.

As a caregiver for someone as helpless as Mom, there is a huge weight of responsibility. There is pressure to advocate, and also pressure to provide the protection and care that is needed. There were times that I felt as though I had failed to protect her.

There was another incident in which I felt responsible. One night earlier that fall, as Lindsey and I were putting Mom to bed, she fell. This was one of our worst fears come true. We were going through the same bedtime routine Mom and her caregivers had been through several thousand times. We hooked the Hoyer lift straps onto the lift, and then we moved Mom several feet from her wheel-chair to hover above the bed. Picture someone in a swing above the bed. I was there beside the bed when the Hoyer straps came off the arm of the lift. She fell. I cried out to Lindsey, who had gone into the bathroom to get something for Mom. I was shaken, but Mom was actually quite calm. She kept reassuring us that she was all right. God was so gracious to us that night. Many times I have prayed, thanking God that Mom was already above the bed when she fell. Had she been over the floor, that night could have had a catastrophic ending. Feeling so responsible for her protection, I felt so guilty.

On Thanksgiving morning, when it was time for our family Christmas gift-exchange, Mom wasn't there in the middle of it. The grandchildren took turns going into her room to thank her for their gifts and to show her what they had opened. During our Thanksgiving dinner, we took turns going in to sit next to her bed. Later that day, we all gathered around her bed to hear Dad read a letter that Mom had dictated days earlier to one of the caregivers. There were many tears shed as Dad read her words aloud to us.

Her letter read,

Dear Family,

Thanksgiving is a special time. We get to say thank-you every day. I know I don't always say it, but I want to say a special thank you to all of you. I want to encourage you to always say thank-you to those you love without hesitation. I have been one of the most fortunate women in the world. I have lived a long healthy life for most of my life. I've gotten to be active and work and help people, and most of all, I have gotten to have a wonderful family. I have had a wonderful husband for forty years whom I love and cherish. I have three beautiful children who married three godly (and beautiful) spouses. They've given me nine beautiful grandchildren—all healthy and happy and lots of fun. They bring me so much joy. We have so much fun together. I can't say enough about you all…and that is a blessing that not everyone has. I pray that you will have the same someday. I count my blessings every day. I had wonderful parents and a brother. Some days you just go back and count the blessings you have and realize how rich you are. No matter how much money you have…it doesn't matter at all. I just wanted to say thanks, and realize that *all* of these blessings come from God, our Father in heaven. And remember, if you have Jesus, you have everything. Without him, you have nothing. I pray for you all every day. I pray that all my grandchildren meet wonderful, godly spouses and enjoy watching their families come together.

Another excerpt says,

I have so much more I want to say. You know the wedding vows, you know, sickness and in health? You have seen Gram in sickness. But I am still in a happy place. My only regret is I want to play with you and be active with you. I want you to know that I love you always and cherish you in my heart forever and ever. I am so thankful for you…my grandchildren, all my children, Doug, I love you all. Thank you for being the family you are. Happy Thanksgiving 2015.

Love,
Gram

On Friday, Todd Teller and Wilson and Pam Benton came over to the house to visit. We have known the Bentons since I was seven years old. Wilson was our first pastor when we moved to Mississippi. Pam and Mom taught me most of the Scripture songs I still remember today, and she took care of me in her home when I had chickenpox as a child. Mom taught their children to play piano and guitar so many years ago. They were dear friends in Cleveland.

Our whole family, Todd, Wilson, and Pam all gathered around Mom's bed. She was in and out of consciousness during their visit. Todd read Scripture and prayed. Wilson prayed for her as he stroked her forehead. I was standing down near the foot of Mom's bed. Pam pulled the covers off Mom's feet and rubbed them the whole time we were around the bed.

On Sunday morning, everyone traveled home. Dad went to church, as did my family. I decided to go and sit with Mom, since it just seemed as though she would not be with us much longer. When I arrived, Annika was sitting by Mom's bedside reading Scripture to her. Mom slipped in and out of fitful sleep, frequently moaning in pain. I read what had been one of my favorite passages throughout her journey, 2 Corinthians 4:16–18:

> Therefore we do not lose heart. Though outwardly we are wasting away, yet inwardly we are being renewed day by day. For our light and momentary troubles are achieving for us an eternal glory that far outweighs them all. So we fix our eyes not on what is seen, but on what is unseen. For what is seen is temporary, but what is unseen is eternal. (NIV)

And then, I continued to read on into chapter 5 and discovered beautiful words that were so relevant to what Mom was going through at the moment. Second Corinthians 5:1–5 says,

> For we know that if the earthly tent we live in is destroyed, we have a building from God, an eternal house in heaven, not built by human hands. Meanwhile we groan, longing to be clothed instead with our heavenly dwelling, because when we are clothed, we will not be found naked. For while we are in this tent, we

groan and are burdened, because we do not wish to be unclothed but to be clothed instead with our heavenly dwelling, so that what is mortal may be swallowed up by life. Now the one who has fashioned us for this very purpose is God, who has given us the Spirit as a deposit, guaranteeing what is to come. (NIV)

What a gift these words were in those moments with Mom! I said, "Mom, this is what is happening right now. You are groaning in your earthly tent, longing and waiting to be clothed in your heavenly one."

*****

On Monday morning, the phone calls began to get hospice orders for Mom. Due to insurance and other issues, it was six on Monday night when the hospice nurse finally arrived. I got to the house at six thirty, and as I looked into Mom's eyes and spoke to her, I could tell she did not recognize me.

I was amazed to see that the nurse had already efficiently set up a makeshift office for herself in Mom's room. As she assessed Mom and listened to her crying out in pain, she was livid that Mom had been in this much pain for so long and that we had not been able to get anyone to listen. She immediately got the order from the hospice physician for morphine for Mom. Then, she called the pharmacy and said, "I'm calling this in for immediate release for morphine." She hung up, looked at Dad, and said, "Go. It will be ready when you get there."

Thirty minutes later, the first dose was pushed through Mom's feeding tube. It was a beautiful, miraculous thing to watch her body and face relax and rest. I sat with Mom and Dad for a while, visited with the caregivers, and went home to my family at around eight thirty.

I had been in the practice of keeping my phone on the bedside table in case Mom and Dad ever needed anything during the night.

At 1:30 a.m. on December 1, I woke to it ringing. I knew before I even answered. When I did answer, Dad was crying on the other end. I was barely able to make out the words, "Jules, Mom just died." Will was awake, and he rolled over and hugged me for a few minutes as I cried. He asked me if I wanted him to come with me. I told him I didn't know how long I would be and that I wanted him to stay with the kids. I quickly dressed and drove across town to their house.

I walked into the bedroom at 2:00 a.m. to hear Dad on the phone with the hospice nurse. Liz was standing at the head of the bed gently brushing Mom's hair. I hugged Dad, and then I kissed Mom on the forehead and stood there hugging Liz as we cried together. I said, "Liz, you saw her through. You took care of her from the beginning to the end."

The hospice nurse arrived shortly after I did. She could tell earlier in the evening that Mom was close to the end, but she had not expected it to happen so quickly. She walked over to Mom to confirm her death. And then I remember Dad asking her if he should turn off her pacer and unhook it. She nodded, and as he unplugged it, he sobbed. That box, along with her ventilator, had given her every single breath for almost ten years.

Dad explained what had transpired in the hours leading up to Mom's death. He said that he had gotten up at midnight to give Mom her second dose of morphine. At around one thirty, he heard her make a strange, gurgling noise. He got up and walked over to her and saw her chest rise and fall one last time. Dad watched her take her last breath. He witnessed the moment she went to be with Jesus.

What Mom's death might eventually look like had always been a fear for me and for others in the family. Because a machine gave her every breath, would it continue to cause her lungs to expand and contract even in the event of heart or multi-organ failure? Would a decision have to be made to turn off her ventilator? Thankfully, this was not how it happened. Even though her pacer was still on, her breathing had stopped. There were no answers as to her cause of death. Ten years is a long period of time for someone to survive as a ventilator-dependent quadriplegic, and it seemed as though her body was just worn out.

Although we only had hospice care for seven hours, it was a tremendous blessing to Mom and to the rest of us. Even though there was only time for Mom to receive two doses of morphine, it allowed her to rest peacefully at the end. She died in her sleep, unaware that she was unable to breathe. We learned from the hospice nurse that if someone died at home and hospice was not involved, the police have to be called to investigate. We were so thankful that God had spared us from the grief that would have come from such a situation.

I'm not sure how long I stayed there by Mom's side, but eventually I decided to go home to try to get some rest. We woke the kids up at the normal time to get ready for school. Will told them that Gram had died during the night, and we gave them each the option of staying home or going to school that day. Emily and William decided to go to school, but Luke and Caleb wanted to be with me.

I got the older two off to school, and not long after I arrived at Mom and Dad's house with the younger two, I received a call from the school that William really wanted to come home. My sweet friend Gigi offered to get William and bring him to me.

I walked into the bedroom, and Mom was gone. Sometime after I had left in the middle of the night, they came to take her body away. Her bed was empty, and so was her wheelchair. The two pieces of furniture she had occupied for the last ten years. Empty.

The kitchen held a different scene altogether. Dad and most of our pastors were gathered around the table planning Mom's funeral service.

The next few days were a bit of a fog. It was a bittersweet time of being so thankful that Mom's suffering was finally over but also missing her presence with us. Thankfully, because of encouragement weeks earlier from my friend Kathy, we had already chosen a funeral home to work with and had met with the funeral planner before Mom died.

Chapter 26

It Is Well, But Is It?

My siblings and their families, as well as some extended family, began to arrive in town as plans continued to be made for the Saturday service. The funeral home was so helpful, as well as the newly formed Bereavement Committee at our church. I have had the privilege of serving on this committee, and our family felt very well cared for on the receiving end.

On Saturday morning, we gathered at the church to spend some time at Mom's open casket before the visitation began. As I stood there, I was struck by the silence around Mom's body in comparison to the sounds that I had associated with her for the past ten years. The sounds of the ventilator forcing air into her lungs, the cough machine that was used to remove obstructions from her airway, the background noise of the television as we went about her morning and evening routines, the beep from her wheelchair every thirty minutes to remind us it was time for another weight shift, the conversation among Mom and the caregivers, the liquids pushed through her feeding tube. And visually, so many things were absent. No feeding tube, no pacer wires coming out of her chest, no pacer control box, no suprapubic catheter, no ostomy bag, no ventilator machine. And to cover the hole where her trach had been, a lovely scarf graced her neck.

The most notable thing, however, was that Mom was no longer at home inside that badly broken body. No longer held captive. Her soul, the part that made her who she was, was clearly gone. This was only the tent where she had lived while on this broken earth.

For the next couple of hours, friends and family filed past the open casket to speak words of comfort to us and to show their support.

Then the service began. It was a time filled with plenty of Mom's favorite music, including "Crown Him with Many Crowns" (Matthew Bridges, 1851), which we had also sung just a year and a half earlier at Mom Mayfield's funeral. Of course, we sang "Whate'er My God Ordains Is Right," as well as "Whom Shall I Fear? (God of Angel Armies)," which had been sung by her bedside just the week before. It was also a time filled with reminders of promises from Scripture. Psalm 139 was read; Mom had memorized it in its entirety during her cancer treatment. My brother Jeff got up and spoke about Mom. I was so proud of him for having the courage to do so.

Our friend Jeannette Leggett sang the song that she and Mom had written during their music therapy sessions together. Mom had titled it, "All Things."

> For from Him and to Him and through Him are
> all things.
> For from Him and to Him and through Him are
> all things.
> To Him be the glory forever! To Him be the glory
> forever!
> Amen, amen!
> All things come to us from our Father above,
> Filtered through His hands of love.
> The good things and the bad are part of His plan.
> In His sovereignty, we can stand.
> For from Him and to Him and through Him are
> all things.
> For from Him and to Him and through Him are
> all things.
> To Him be the glory forever! To Him be the glory
> forever!

Amen, amen!
For from Him and to Him and through Him are
    all things.
Amen, amen!

On Monday, December 7, 2015, our extended family, some caregivers, and friends gathered at the cemetery to bury Mom. It was a cold, rather gloomy day, which seemed like the perfect setting. But the words David Filson spoke at the graveside were life-giving. He talked about how we weren't just burying a body, we were making a resurrection deposit for safekeeping until that great resurrection day. And he also said, "It's very quiet out here in the cemetery now. But this is resurrection ground, and on that day, this place will be filled with the loud sound and rejoicing of resurrection." I reflect on these words every time I'm in a cemetery.

The inscription on Mom's headstone is short and simple but profound: *It is well with my soul.* Because Dad served in the Air Force, she is buried in the lovely grounds of the Middle Tennessee Veterans' Cemetery. The headstones are all rather small and uniform in size, which means there is only space for a short inscription. I went with Dad to order the headstone, and they handed us a book with samples for inscriptions. Nothing sounded right until we got to *It is well with my soul.* We immediately knew this was the perfect one for Mom. The Lord had preserved her faith throughout her journey of suffering, and it was also one of her favorite hymns.

It Is Well with My Soul

When peace like a river attendeth my way,
When sorrows like sea billows roll;
Whatever my lot, thou hast taught me to say,
It is well, it is well with my soul.

Though Satan should buffet, though trials should
    come,
Let this blest assurance control,

That Christ has regarded my helpless estate,
And has shed his own blood for my soul.

My sin—O the bliss of this glorious thought!
My sin, not in part, but the whole,
Is nailed to the cross and I bear it no more;
Praise the Lord, praise the Lord, O my soul!

This last verse I can never sing without a lump in my throat, or without crying.

O Lord, haste the day when the faith shall be
    sight,
The clouds be rolled back as a scroll,
The trump shall resound, and the Lord shall
    descend,
Even so—it is well with my soul.

(Horatio G. Spafford, 1873)

Over the next few days, we said goodbye to family knowing that, Lord willing, we would gather together again for holidays and special occasions. We also said the difficult goodbyes to caregivers, not knowing when or if we would see them again. They had become family to us. Mom was the reason they were in our lives, and now Mom was gone.

Chapter 27

Hiking toward Hope

That December was sad and quiet, with all the planning done and family and caregivers gone. And while I was so thankful that Mom's suffering was over, I missed her. I felt myself sinking further into depression. There were a few times in the weeks following Mom's death that I crawled into bed intending to just rest for a bit, but I stayed there awake for hours, unable to will myself to get up and out of bed.

Will was very kind and understanding, but he also used some tough love. I am so thankful that he did this on several occasions. I remember one particular Sunday afternoon, I crawled into bed after church and lunch. I stayed there for probably four or five hours. Will came in a couple of times to tell me it was time to get up. I rolled over and ignored him. He finally came back and said, "Come on, we're going for a walk. It's time to get out of bed." He stood there until I got up, and we did go for a walk.

This was a turning point for me. That day, I decided to no longer rest in my bed during the day. This has become important for me in my struggle with depression. If I feel like I need to rest during the day, I lie down on the sofa with a book or a movie with the kids.

I also continued to go to counseling for the next few months. Margaret helped me to continue to work through my grief and depression, and she continued to remind me that it was really important for me to pursue a new skill in the arts. I just could not imagine finding the energy to learn something new, so I continued to do nothing about it. And, most importantly, she continued to remind me of God's promises.

By early summer, with the encouragement of Will, I was able to gradually come off my antidepressants. I realize there are those who need to stay on them. Everyone is different. I am thankful I was able to come off them, but if needed, I wouldn't hesitate to take them again. I no longer associate shame with taking medications for depression and anxiety.

In the fall, Will and I were blessed to be able to take another hiking trip together, and Dad was willing to stay with our kids. This time, we spent a week in the Canadian Rockies. The scenery in Banff and Yoho National Parks is absolutely breathtaking, the most beautiful mountains I have ever visited. We reached the summit of Mount Bourgeau in a blizzard, hiked along the edges of glaciers on the Iceline Trail, and paddled on the most gorgeous water on Emerald Lake.

On one of our hikes, it was very cloudy as we ascended the trail, making it impossible for us to take in the panoramic views. We could only see the trail in front of us and the trees around us. Suddenly, the clouds parted for a few minutes to reveal a spectacular sight. Just a few feet to the left of the trail, there was an impressive vertical drop, and beyond the chasm rose an impressive range of snowcapped mountains! It felt as though God had pulled the curtains back to give us a glimpse of the big picture around us. To me, this seemed like a good metaphor for what our journey through life can be.

Quite often, we are called to faithfully trudge along our path, unaware of what is around us. Sometimes God parts the curtains to give us a glimpse of the beautiful big picture we are a small part of. But the journey is not about us; it is about Jesus. The goal and reward are not success and happiness; the reward is him. Hebrews uses a race metaphor for the Christian life:

> Therefore, since we are surrounded by such
> a great cloud of witnesses, let us throw off every-
> thing that hinders and the sin that so easily entan-
> gles, and let us run with perseverance the race

marked out for us. Let us fix our eyes on Jesus, the author and perfecter of our faith, who for the joy set before him endured the cross, scorning its shame, and sat down at the right hand of the throne of God. Consider him who endured such opposition from sinful men, so that you will not grow weary and lose heart. (Hebrews 12:1–3 NIV)

On our hikes at altitude, we grew weary from our heavy packs full of water and supplies. Had we thrown them off, we might have been able to breathe easier and make better time. Although our hiking supplies were necessary, there are so many things in this life that weigh us down spiritually. The cares of this world and our sin weigh us down and distract us from keeping our eyes on Jesus.

We hiked a total of sixty miles that week, sometimes talking about the enormous losses of the last couple of years, but mostly we hiked in silence. This is the beauty of a marriage between two introverts!

As our senses took in all that those mountains had to offer, God was bringing some healing. The mountain views, the sunshine on our faces, the peaceful silence around us, the sound of a waterfall, the crisp mountain air filling our lungs, snowflakes hitting our faces, the smell of evergreens, the rhythm of our footfalls: God was the maker of all these things. As Hebrews 1:3 says, "He (Jesus) is the radiance of the glory of God and the exact imprint of his nature, and he upholds the universe by the word of his power" (ESV). It is amazing. He created everything with his words, and the word of his power continues to hold it all together, including his children. He has not left us, and he never will. Deuteronomy 31:8 says, "It is the Lord who goes before you. He will be with you; he will not leave you or forsake you. Do not fear or be dismayed" (ESV).

In November of that year, 2016, two years after I went to counseling for the first time, I began taking cello lessons. This was something I had wanted to do for years, but I just didn't have the mental energy or the courage. Because Margaret had repeatedly reminded me of the importance of such a pursuit, I sent her a text to let her know that I had finally been brave enough to do it. Music had always been such an important part of my life, and this new challenge did prove to be beneficial to my mental health. My teacher, Elizabeth, is a gifted performer and teacher, and the time I spend with her each week is a gift.

In the spring of 2017, beautiful tulips came up in our yard. The bulbs had been a gift from a dear friend after Mom died. A few days later, we had an unusual March snow. I looked out in the yard and saw a strange sight. There was one lone tulip still standing strong, defiant against the snow and cold. Its lovely pink bloom looked like a cup holding a large snowball. As I observed this unusual sight, God lifted more of my depression and awakened some hope in my soul. I began to think about Jesus being our hope in the winter seasons of life that sometimes come. I snapped a picture, and then went inside and wrote a short poem to capture my thoughts.

Hope

New Spring life, standing its ground, holding fast
Against Winter's final attempt at a chilling blast.
Have hope! The winter of the soul will not last,
For Jesus Christ, on our behalf, is holding fast.

Chapter 28

Doubt, Faith, and Idols

There are so many times in life when we all ask, "What if?" For me, these tragic events with our parents have brought out many of those questions.

There are the what-ifs that put me in the place of God, leading to a "God complex," effectively letting him know that had I been in control, things would have ended much better. There are the what-ifs that tell me that if I had made better decisions, there would have been a better outcome. Who do I think I am? Do I honestly think that I have the power to change outcomes and events? Do I really believe that my different actions or words can thwart the plan of God? If I truly believe that God is sovereign over all things, do I trust that maybe he knows things I don't? He is God, and he gets to see the big picture that we do not see. He may choose to reveal it to us one day, but he may not.

On December 25, 2005, what if I had not insisted on taking a picture of the kids before leaving for church, or there hadn't been a clogged toilet, or Mom had ridden in our car, or we had just decided to relax at home on Christmas morning instead of going to church, or both cars left just a few minutes earlier or later?

Leading up to the events of April 30, 2014, what if we had known just how sick Will's dad was, or I did take the kids to visit them over spring break, or we had pressed Mom more about specifics on how Dad was doing, or we went to Jackson to check on them after

Dad wandered off the night of April 28? What if Dad had not been beaten and his care neglected while he was in jail? Would he still be alive and here with us?

The enemy loves for us to go down this road of questioning. It causes us to question if God really cares and is sovereign, and Satan also uses it to heap enormous guilt upon us.

Then there are the what-ifs that cause me to see God's hand at work, and I realize that he is sovereign and ever-present with us in the valleys and the darkness.

On December 25, 2005, what if the wreck had happened a day later and Will had not been there to perform rescue breathing on Mom?

We had come to Atlanta in two cars because Will had to leave the day after Christmas to get home to take call for the practice. We came around the curve in the road less than a minute after the accident, and Will was able to begin rescue breathing on Mom very quickly.

What if so many helpers had not stopped to help, or the ambulances hadn't arrived so quickly to get Mom intubated, or Jeff and Wendy and their children had been gravely injured, or Mom had died at the scene, or Susan and Todd had been unable to move in to take care of Mom, or we had not been able to find additional caregivers, or there hadn't been a settlement to provide financially for Mom's care, or Mom and Dad still lived in a small town that did not have the medical resources for Mom's care?

And there are the questions about the events of April 30, 2014 and the weeks following. What if the shooting had occurred a few days earlier, when grandchildren were staying with them, or a few days later, when Mom's sisters were there? What if Dad had survived long enough for the case to go to trial, or Dad remembered what he did, or he had been healthy enough to stay in jail longer than four days? What if Pastor Steve had not lovingly taken upon himself the task of cleaning up the scene of the shooting before any family arrived at the house? What if we did not have the information from the 911 call and the police report, the gift of information that let us know that Dad did not intend to kill his dear wife? He said he had shot a woman who was after him and that he couldn't find his wife.

*****

God has sustained us and held us by his grace, even if from our perspective, it seemed like it was a very thin strand of grace at times. But these losses did not get wrapped up all nicely with a bow in the end. We still do not understand how God works all things together for our good in these situations. We may not see it until heaven, and maybe not even then.

Isaiah 55:8–9 says, "For my thoughts are not your thoughts, neither are your ways my ways, declares the Lord. As the heavens are higher than the earth, so are my ways higher than your ways and my thoughts than your thoughts" (NIV).

In the book of Job, we see a man who suffered greatly, losing his possessions, all ten of his children at once, and eventually his health. Chapter 1, verse 20 tells us Job's response: "Then Job arose and tore his robe and shaved his head and fell on the ground and worshiped" (ESV). This is astounding to me.

Later in the account, we do learn that Job has questions for God and that he voices his despair. He even laments that he was born, saying, "Why did I not die at birth, come out of the womb and expire?" (Job 3:11 ESV). After approaching God with many questions, chapter 38 of the Book of Job begins with this:

> Then the Lord answered Job out of the whirlwind and said: "Who is this that darkens counsel by words without knowledge? Dress for action like a man; I will question you, and you make it known to me. Where were you when I laid the foundation of the earth? Tell me, if you have understanding. Who determined its measurements—surely you know!" (ESV)

Then in Job chapter 40:

> And the Lord said to Job: "Shall a fault-finder contend with the Almighty? He who argues with God, let him answer it." Then Job answered the Lord and said: "Behold, I am of small account: what shall I answer you? I lay my hand on my mouth. I have spoken once, and I will not answer; twice, but I will proceed no further." (ESV)

And then God continues again with the same line of questioning Job as before. God never abandoned Job, but God did rebuke him and remind him that he is God even if Job did not understand his ways.

God has not promised anywhere in his Word that we will understand his ways. He just calls us to believe him.

*****

Throughout these ordeals, as our faith has been tested and stretched, God has begun to reveal to us what some of our idols are. It is just the tip of the iceberg, and we have much more to learn.

When we think of an idol, we often picture someone worshipping and bowing down to a statue. While that is a type of idol, there are also idols we manufacture in our own hearts. An idol can be anything, seen or unseen, that takes the place of God in our hearts. Long ago, John Calvin said, "Man's nature is a perpetual factory of idols."

Soon after the death of his parents, Will shared with me what God was teaching him about his idols. One idol he felt that God had torn down for him was the idol of expectation that God owes us a good death. If we live a quiet, faithful life as a follower of Jesus, then we are deserving of a death that reflects that. A peaceful, dignified death with loved ones around the deathbed singing hymns and ushering us into heaven. There are times when this happens, and it is a beautiful gift, but God doesn't owe us this.

This is faulty thinking and theology. We think of ourselves as faithful to God, when God is the one who is faithful to us. And of course, God does not owe us anything. Nothing.

So this was a major paradigm shift in our thinking. Why would God allow Mom and Dad Mayfield to die in such tragic ways? Will's parents belonged to Jesus, they sought to live for him, and they lived quiet, faithful lives. The horrific tragedy that took them home looked nothing like the way they had lived their lives. And I wanted to defend them to people who didn't know them and to the media who portrayed them as something other than who they really were. This was the beginning of my realizing that this is where faith in God's plan has to begin… "Abraham believed God." I knew God was calling me to believe him in this, to believe that he is who he says he is in the Bible.

Another of Will's idols that God was revealing to him was that of delayed gratification. Will's dad had worked hard during his career, and now should have been the time that he and Mom enjoyed their retirement years together. Will and I have both learned through this that we are not promised tomorrow.

We are learning that today is a gift, and we should live fully present in it, as though it may be our last. Maybe this is why we are not good at planning events or vacations months or even years ahead of time. We tend to be late or last-minute planners.

Because he does not get vacation days, Will used to have a difficult time taking time off from work. When he takes time off, he loses money since he is not generating any income while continuing to pay his overhead and employees. Because of these sudden losses in recent years, we have decided to go ahead and take vacations now when we are able and if we have the resources, instead of planning five or ten years down the road.

God was also revealing some of my idols to me. Family was a huge one, and I realized that it had been since Will and I married. Things were so wonderful. We had parents who loved one another and had good marriages. We celebrated holidays and other occasions together with our extended families. We all genuinely enjoyed being together. Everyone was healthy and happy. Family is a wonderful gift, but I realized it was something I worshiped.

I also realized that I had made Will and our marriage an idol. I had expected him to be my Jesus. I was looking to him to meet my needs that can only be met by Christ, and when these tragedies hit us hard, it became clear to me.

Right before Mom's cancer diagnosis, I had told Will that I didn't know what I would do without my mom if something happened to her. This is the idol of family. What I should be asking is, "What would I do without Jesus? Is Jesus alone enough for me?" Because of his death and resurrection on behalf of his children, thankfully I will never know what it would be like to have to live without Jesus.

Another of my idols was comfort. I was doing all I could to create a comfortable existence here instead of longing for my heavenly home. We are called to be content here, not complacent and comfortable.

The desire to be in control is a huge idol of mine. Sinking into the deep hole of depression and experiencing panic attacks left me feeling out of control. Maybe God brought me to that point of despair to remind me of my need for him. He has always been sovereign over the events in my life and has always known the number of hairs on my head, but struggling with depression has certainly made me more aware of my dependence on him.

Not long after Mom's accident, I received an email from our friend Sue Jakes. I will never forget how she signed it: "In His grip, Sue." Those three little words changed my perspective. We so often think we are desperately holding on to Jesus for dear life, and that it's all over if we let go. So much energy is spent striving and controlling, when instead he invites us to rest "in His grip." Jesus is the one who holds and sustains us.

Another idol is wanting to protect my children from suffering; to protect their innocence. I would have never chosen for them to be at the scene of Gram's accident. We never dreamed we would have to tell them that Pop shot Grandmother, or that we would take them into a hospital room where they would see Pop handcuffed to the bed. I never longed for family meals to be a time when my kids would watch my mom repeatedly choke on food that lodged in her trach. However, suffering has given them compassion for others who are hurting. I pray that the suffering they have endured and witnessed will increase their desire to know Jesus more, and that it will also give them a greater longing to be with him in heaven.

Distraction and escape are an idol for me. I love planning the next family vacation and deciding what novel to get lost in, while ignoring regular Bible reading and prayer. While family vacations are wonderful, they can sometimes become more important to me than God. I can so often become distracted from God and his faithfulness as I long for the next thing to happen.

I also realized that after Mom's accident, I did not expect any other trials. God had given us this one, awful tragedy, I thought, and we would not experience anything like this again. This is also an idol of mine. Mom's accident was the first major trial I had experienced in life, and I really thought that would be it. So when Will's parents died, I felt like God had somehow failed us. We had already had our suffering. I am not sure why I thought this way, but I have not seen anywhere in Scripture that substantiates my thought process. I am learning that everyone in this world either has experienced or will experience heartache, and it is not all equal. Some have more, some have less. But none of us will ever experience suffering as severe as what Jesus went through for us.

Chapter 29

Hard-Pressed but Not Crushed

We are hard-pressed on every side, but not crushed; perplexed, but not in despair; persecuted, but not abandoned; struck down, but not destroyed. We always carry around in our body the death of Jesus, so that the life of Jesus may also be revealed in our body.

—2 Corinthians 4:8–10 (NIV)

I have read this passage many times but have always seen it as being about our human suffering. It is, but I recently realized I have been missing that it is really about Jesus. Yes, we are hard-pressed, perplexed, persecuted, and struck down. But Jesus was in despair, asking the Father to let the cup pass from him. He was crushed and destroyed on the cross for us, and his Father abandoned him there.

There is a fascinating phenomenon that occurs in glacial lakes all over the world, and it allows our eyes to see the most amazing hues of blues and greens. One place this occurs is in the Canadian Rockies, in Banff and Yoho National Parks.

There is a brutal, violent process that happens on the mountain high above the lake to create the breathtaking beauty below. The mountain rock is literally crushed by the weight of the glacier that sits on it. As the glacier shifts and settles, the rock beneath is pulverized into a fine rock flour or glacial silt. In the springtime, the glacier begins to thaw, and the runoff washes the silt down into the lake below. The rock flour is suspended in the lake water, giving it a cloudy appearance.

The lake water absorbs the reds, yellows, and oranges of the spectrum, while the silt absorbs the indigo and purple light waves of the spectrum. So when the sunlight hits the water, greens and blues are reflected. The lake has no spectacular beauty in and of itself. Instead, it reflects the beauty of the rock flour within it, caused by the crushing of the weight of the glacier above.

In a similar way, our beauty comes not from us but from Jesus. As the mountain is crushed by the weight of the glacier, so Jesus was crushed for our iniquities. Like the rock flour rests in the lake, he was placed in a tomb. The sun shines on the glacial lake, reflecting spectacular greens and blues. When Jesus was resurrected on the third day, he brought light back to a dark and hurting world. We have been given the gift of being made beautiful through Jesus's suffering and resurrection.

Suffering is intense. It hurts. And it can seem permanent, but the Bible is clear that it is not. It is temporary. In fact, it even says that our sufferings cannot even compare to the glory that awaits us. What? Is God making light of our suffering, saying that it is really not a big deal? Absolutely not.

In the short thirty-three years or so that Jesus walked this earth in the flesh, he suffered in every way. He left heaven to become "Immanuel," God with us. He suffered more than any of us ever will, taking on all our sin and bearing the full wrath of his Father. Jesus was unattractive, rejected, despised, homeless, mocked, and beaten, and he died a violent death for crimes he didn't commit.

Isaiah 53:2–6 says,

> He had no form or majesty that we should look at him, and no beauty that we should desire him. He was despised and rejected by men, a man of sorrows and acquainted with grief; and as one from whom men hide their faces he was despised, and we esteemed him not. Surely he has borne our griefs and carried our sorrows; yet

we esteemed him stricken, smitten by God, and afflicted. But he was pierced for our transgressions; he was crushed for our iniquities; upon him was the chastisement that brought us peace, and with his wounds we are healed. All we like sheep have gone astray; we have turned—every one—to his own way; and the Lord has laid on him the iniquity of us all. (ESV)

We have a Savior who understands. He can truly empathize with any suffering we may encounter in this fallen world. Do I sometimes question him and accuse him of giving us more than we can take? Absolutely, but then I have to remind myself of his own suffering, and I am again reminded that he does understand. In the weight of our grief in our tragedies, the incarnation of Jesus Christ has brought me the most comfort. That he would willingly leave glory, take on flesh, live among us, suffer, and die for us is truly astounding. He was not just "God with us" until he went back to heaven. He continues to be Immanuel through the indwelling of the Holy Spirit in those who belong to him.

I had many moments during our tragedies when I could not feel his presence in the moment. I cried out to him and wondered where he was, but later, as I have reflected on those times, I can see the evidence that he was there with me. My emotions deceive me, and I cannot depend on whether or not I can feel that he is there. Again, it comes back to choosing to believe in him and in his promise to never leave us.

The Bible also tells us that Jesus endured the suffering he did "for the joy set before him." We, his children, are that joy!

Chapter 30

Hurt, Help, and Gratitude

When there has been catastrophic loss and ongoing, relentless suffering, we wonder what we should say and do. In spite of best intentions, there are words and deeds that can be very hurtful, and I know I have been guilty of unintentionally hurting others in these ways at times. Then there are words and actions that are truly a balm. We have been on the receiving end of both from friends and even strangers, and thankfully, we were helped more than hurt over the years. I pray to follow in the steps of those who showed great kindness and empathy to our family.

Very soon after Mom's injury, a well-meaning friend or two shared with Mom that they knew she would walk again, on this side of heaven. Oh, how painful this can be for the person who is suffering to hear! Even if you believe God has told you something like that directly (which I don't believe he does), it may be best to just keep that to yourself. Mom did not walk again on this side of heaven. She never even took a single breath without a machine doing it for her.

Mom also heard people say that they wished they could be in her condition because it gave her a closer walk with the Lord. Also, the words, "I don't know how you do it!" or "I could never do that" were painful to hear. It made it sound like it was something she chose to do, or like they would just refuse to do it if it happened to them. The truth is that none of us can imagine how we would be able to handle significant suffering when it comes. God will provide sufficient grace when the time comes, just as he gives us what we need every day.

When Mom was out and about, she quite often was the recipient of many stares, which was somewhat understandable given the large wheelchair and all her machines. Some glances were just out of curiosity, but some were out of annoyance for the disruptions Mom and her caregivers caused. In quiet settings like concerts, church, restaurants, and sometimes movies, the noises seemed amplified: the beeping of her weight shift reminder every thirty seconds, the sound of the ventilator, the getting up and leaving to take care of breathing needs or the ostomy bag or catheter, and the sound of stirring of medications and pushing them through her feeding tube.

After the death of Will's parents, I occasionally heard, "Well, at least things can't get any worse." This is just not true. God is sovereign, and he sustains us, but the fact is that from our human perspective, things can always get worse.

What we have not needed is for people to encourage us to "move on," and thankfully we have had very little of that. The fact is, we don't "get over" the loss of people we love, and sudden, tragic loss adds another dimension to the grief.

What we *have* needed is for people to remember our parents, as well as the anguish we went through. Remembering and acknowledging can be through simple words or by the gift of time. We have been blessed and carried by beautiful acts and words of love so many times that the following examples barely scratch the surface.

Susan Wolters, who was one of Mom's closest friends for many years (and also my friend), will often send me a text when we sing a hymn in church that reminds her of Mom. She also shares stories about Mom and favorite memories with me. It is such a gift to have a dear friend with a long history with our family, a friend who knew Mom for years and years before she was injured.

My friend Garland called me probably six months after the shooting. She said something like, "Julie, I hesitated to call because I didn't want to bring it up and remind you. But I just wanted to check on you all." I assured her that she had not caused any pain by bringing it up because it was always at the forefront of our minds. Instead, it brought me great comfort that she remembered us.

A little while after my mom died, Scott and Patti spent time with us over dinner because they just wanted to check in and see how we were doing in our grief. They remembered us. Kristin and Catha continue to love me and talk me through holidays and other hard times. They remember. My friend Susan walks and hikes miles with me, listening to me continue to process grief. She remembers.

We had dinner with Patrick and Susan recently. Patrick brought up my Mom and asked, "What you went through with your mom was really extreme. How would you say it has changed you?" It was such a great question that it stopped me in my tracks. It really made me think to name the hard but also good ways that it has changed me. We always seem to ask people, "How are you doing?" which is not a terrible question. But his question acknowledged that these huge events do change us. We often expect and want someone to remain the same person, even after a horrific event. Will and I are not the same people we were before these tragedies that took our parents. We are different in some sad ways, but we have also changed in some beautiful ways as God has brought some beauty from the ashes. I hope that I will remember to ask others the question Patrick asked.

I met my precious friend Shannon not long after the shooting. I just launched right into telling her that our family had just had some tragic loss. She asked and wanted to know the story. She listened and then she gave me the privilege of hearing her painful story. Her dear parents had died together in a motorcycle accident the summer following Mom's accident. That day, God gave me a soul sister, and we love each other through holidays, Grandparents Day, and ordinary days. She remembers.

I think of my friend Kellie, who is so welcoming and allows me to be vulnerable. We have had beautiful conversations over the years in which she balances grief and hope with such grace.

While we have received so much support from friends, I have been guilty of expecting people to meet needs in ways that only Jesus can. There were times I was hurt because friends and family did not meet those expectations. Yes, God does use others in our lives, but he is the great physician and the only one capable of bringing healing in suffering. Expecting others to be my Jesus is not fair to them, and it isn't good for my soul. There is only one Jesus.

There is a strong connection between Jackson, Mississippi, and Nashville, Tennessee. Will and I occasionally run into and meet people who are old friends or acquaintances of him and his family, or sometimes people we don't know or remember. It is sweet when they mention Will's parents, how they knew them, and the influence they had on them. These seemingly insignificant interactions mean so much to us. The memories and remembrances they share are treasures.

*****

Just staying engaged and active in the church has been extremely important for us. Worshiping with our church family every Sunday is not only necessary, we look forward to it all week long. No, our church isn't perfect, and yes, the church is full of hypocrites, including me! But Jesus called the church his bride, and in spite of all her imperfections, he loves her anyway.

All the aspects of Sunday worship are vital: the preaching of the Word, singing, praying, fellowship, and celebrating the sacraments together. A few years ago, our church changed the way we take the Lord's Supper, and it has been a huge blessing. Every Sunday, we all go forward to the tables, just like many other churches do. Will has helped me appreciate it even more through the observations he has shared. He loves to watch everyone go forward, and he says that everyone does so with a limp. He says, "Everyone has a limp. Some have literal limps and have to be helped to the table. Others have limps that we cannot see—loss, heartache, illness, broken relationships, and sin. But we're all broken and going to the same place to find hope."

We *need* to be in relationship with God's people! The ladies in my Tuesday morning Bible study small group continue to be a lifeline for me. They are extraordinarily brave as they share the real struggles, heartaches, and joys of their lives, and I am better for it as they challenge me to do the same. Our Sunday night small group of couples is a wonderful group, and we are challenged to dig into the Scriptures and pray together.

Another thing I have discovered we need in our own grief is to serve and love others through their own suffering. We have learned how to do so through these friends and many others who ministered to us. Also, I have found that through our own suffering, I have become more aware and sensitive to the suffering of those around me. Mom's injury and the tragedy of losing Will's parents have given me an empathy that I did not have before. Sometimes this involves just listening, and other times it involves action. The Bible calls us to "weep with those who weep" (Romans 12:15 ESV). Also, 2 Corinthians 1:3–5 says, "Praise be to the God and Father of our Lord Jesus Christ, the Father of compassion and the God of all comfort, who comforts us in all our troubles, so that we can comfort those in any trouble with the comfort we ourselves have received from God. For just as the sufferings of Christ flow over into our lives, so also through Christ our comfort overflows" (NIV).

Will spends time serving patients at Siloam health clinic in Nashville every month. Siloam is a wonderful organization that provides health care to refugees and others in our area who do not have insurance or who lack access to health care for some other reason. He treats patients in their orthopaedic clinic once a month, sometimes communicating through an interpreter.

Especially because of what we went through with my mom, our family has been drawn to the special needs ministry at our church. Our church hosts Special Saturday once a month during the school year and Very Special Bible School for three days in the summers. Children with disabilities and their siblings from our church and the Nashville area come for a morning of Bible stories, music, crafts, and recreation. It provides a much-needed respite for their parents for a few hours. Volunteers get to serve as buddies to the children. It is a beautiful time of worshiping God together, and a celebration of the fact that we are all made in his image. To me, it's a picture of the body of Christ, a reminder that we are all broken in different ways and that we need one another.

I love all my friends from the special needs ministry, but Abby is my friend I am with most often. I also have the privilege of being her buddy during the Sunday school hour once or twice a month. Abby is a beautiful, spunky, loving teenage girl. She is nonverbal, but that does not mean she is unable to communicate! She communicates very well with a whole lot of body language and a little signing. Abby has a smile and a belly laugh that are contagious and can light up a room. She loves music, and she loves to dance and make very happy noises during her favorite songs. Some songs make her calm and contemplative, and I love to watch her face and wonder what she is thinking. I have learned so much having this young lady as my friend. And there is a bonus; her awesome mom, Cheri, has become a dear friend of mine! Abby is one of the first people I want to find in heaven because I cannot wait to have a conversation with her!

These families in our special needs ministry go through a lot, and I don't understand why some families suffer more than others. I just know we are all called to help each other along this side of heaven.

*****

It is amazing how the practice of gratitude changes us and gives us hope for today and for the future. There are many psalms of praise that recall the many works of God. Psalm 136:1, for example, says, "Give thanks to the Lord, for he is good, for his steadfast love endures forever." It goes on to list many of the wonders God performed for his people, each one followed by, "for his steadfast love endures forever." Here are just a few of his works the psalmist calls to mind: "To him who by understanding made the heavens" (verse 5), "to him who divided the Red Sea in two, and made Israel pass through the midst of it, but overthrew Pharaoh and his host in the Red Sea, to him who led his people through the wilderness" (verses 13–16 ESV).

Paul, in his first letter to the Thessalonians, writes to encourage believers in their faith and in godly living. He includes many instructions, but in Chapter 5:16–18, he specifically addresses the practice of thankfulness: "Rejoice always, pray without ceasing, give thanks in all circumstances; for this is the will of God in Christ Jesus for you" (ESV).

The use of the word *in* is significant here. In every translation I read, it says give thanks *in* all circumstances, not *for* all circumstances. Evil and suffering are a result of the fall, so it would be strange, or I would venture to say even wrong, to thank God for certain things as though he were the author and giver of them. Yes, God is absolutely sovereign, and he ordains and allows events and suffering. I do not believe God calls us to thank him for things that grieve him. We would never dream of thanking him for murder, abuse, slavery, or childhood cancer.

However, we are called to thank him *in* all circumstances. During Mom's ten years as a quadriplegic, she was thankful, even in her circumstances. She was thankful for God's provision, protection, and for what she learned about him and his sustaining grace in the midst of her daily suffering.

The loss of Will's parents has been harder for me in terms of understanding how to be thankful in such a horrific situation. Obviously, it would be strange to thank God that Will's dear father shot and killed his wonderful wife. Even being thankful *in* it has been a stretch. But here we are years later, and God has sustained our faith, and that is a gift for which we can give thanks. We are thankful that Will's mother went quickly to be with Jesus, and that his dad is free in heaven instead of locked up in prison.

Charles Spurgeon, in his book *Morning and Evening*, paints the most beautiful word picture in his devotional based on Isaiah 63:7: "I will recount the steadfast love of the Lord, the praises of the Lord, according to all that the Lord has granted us" (ESV). Spurgeon says this: "Arise, go to the river of thine experience, and pull up a few bulrushes, and plait them into an ark, wherein thine infant-faith may float safely on the stream." And then, "Go back, then, a little way to the choice mercies of yesterday, and though all may be dark now, light up the lamps of the past, they shall glitter through the darkness, and thou shalt trust in the Lord till the day break and the shadows flee away" (p. 50).

Oh, how the "lamps of the past" are full of "choice mercies of yesterday." There are numerous ways God has shown his love toward Will and me in the years we have been given so far. Of course, the most beautiful kindness he has shown is giving us relationship with himself. When I think about our parents with a heart of gratitude, what a multitude of beautiful memories flood my mind. I'm thankful Will and I were born into Christian homes and to parents who loved us and wanted the best for us. I am thankful for the years I had my mom and that she was able to play with and hold her grandchildren for a few years. I am thankful for the eighteen years that I knew Will's parents. His mother welcomed me as a daughter, and what a faithful, loving wife and caregiver she was. She loved her grandchildren dearly and loved every minute she spent with them. I am grateful for the times I got to talk to Will's dad as we washed and dried dishes together after family meals. He was characterized by a quiet, gentle faithfulness, and I am proud to call Bill Mayfield my father-in-law. I am grateful that Will inherited his Dad's disposition, and that both he and our son William share Dad's name.

Chapter 31

Grief and Celebration

Grief is very real, and though it changes over the years, it remains. In many cases, it will remain until we are whole and with Jesus. It is also very strange and can hit us out of nowhere, surprising us with powerful blows. Then sometimes, it is followed by equally powerful waves of peace and hope.

One such time happened about a year and a half after my mom's death. Emily and I went away to Orlando for a fun mother-daughter weekend. We spent time at Disney World and Universal Studios doing all her favorite things.

She had made a plan for every hour of every day, prioritizing attractions. Our morning at Magic Kingdom was a little discouraging, as her favorite rides were breaking down. We stood in line for her absolute favorite, "It's a Small World," for at least thirty minutes, and the line wasn't moving. We were soon told that the ride was temporarily closed, as no boats had been loaded in the past half hour. We left the line and decided that we would try again after visiting other parts of the park.

When we did go back later, the wait was around an hour. Discouraged, we got at the end of the long line, where a dear cast member, an older gentleman, began a conversation with us. He asked how we were enjoying our time in the park, and we shared that we were having difficulty finding attractions that were functioning. He then said, "Follow me." He walked us up to the FastPass line and told them to let us through. We thanked him, and then I began to cry. It wasn't just a little cry; I sobbed like a baby. Emily hugged me and patted my arm as we waited to board our boat. I could not stop sobbing. I sobbed through the whole fifteen-minute ride, and after that, for another twenty minutes as we walked around the park.

Sweet Emily was so kind, but I felt terrible. She kept saying, "Mom, why are you still crying? It's gonna be okay. We're at Disney World! This is supposed to be happy and fun." So I explained to her what I thought had caused such a visceral response. When that precious older man had shown us such kindness to help us get onto the ride, it triggered a memory of Mom getting on "It's a Small World" six years earlier. The Cast Members stopped the ride when the wheelchair-accessible boat came around, and a small army of them worked to get her onto the boat so that she could experience it with her family. So when Emily and I were shown kindness at the same place it had been shown to my sweet mom, it brought up a flood of grief; it was a visceral response that took over my whole being. Then, later in the day, the grief left. It was replaced with the joy that came from gratitude; gratitude that we had that experience with Mom years earlier, as well as gratitude for the precious gift of this time with my daughter.

I have learned how important it is to let people grieve how they need to grieve instead of how we would prefer that they grieve. Seeing people grieve can make us uncomfortable. Sometimes we want to correct people in their grief and let them know how and what they should be doing. It is actually possible, after some time has gone by, to simultaneously validate someone's grief and remind them of God's care and promises.

Being honest about grief and suffering is important. So often, we can be concerned about how people perceive us grieving, and Christians especially feel as though we need to be a witness to those watching us grieve. I have heard people talk about how they feel they have a platform, and they need to be careful to be a good witness to those watching. While I understand the desire to grieve well, I think it is extremely important for people to see us grieving honestly. Hiding pain while sharing platitudes is misleading.

*****

Christmas continues to be a rather difficult and sad time. Every Christmas morning, it's hard not to think about December 25, 2005, when two cars collided on that road, changing Mom's life, as well as the lives of the rest of the family. And now that she is gone, her absence is felt every day, and especially at times that extended families get together to celebrate.

Of course, the tragic loss of Will's parents also contributes to the sadness. Their absence during these times is painfully palpable.

The music of the season dredges up so much grief, but also hope. Mom is no longer here, directing her boys' choir or the children's choirs of their churches. Will's parents' voices are absent from their church choir. Mom Mayfield is no longer directing the glorious handbell choir, and Dad Mayfield's trumpet is silent.

Hope comes when I'm reminded of the cloud of witnesses from Hebrews, and I know we are not worshiping alone. It also comes from the music made from those of us who are still here. Will singing in the choir, and Dad playing timpani in church. Emily singing and playing the piano. There is a huge pile of instruments in our living room. Caleb plays Will's old trumpet; Will and William play guitar; Luke plays violin, viola, and saxophone. I have kept up my flute and am continuing with cello. And it is not entirely true that Dad Mayfield's trumpet is silent. We have it, and Will now plays it.

The music I memorized in the past drifts into my conscience, especially the hymns I learned and memorized as a child. My love of hymns came from our church in Cleveland, where we had hymns as a part of our Sunday night service every week. We had the privilege of requesting hymns, and almost every week, a child's hand would shoot up into the air to request no. 500, "When the Roll Is Called up Yonder." I also remember Mom regularly requesting "A Mighty Fortress Is Our God."

Will and I had the privilege of singing Brahms's "Requiem" at First Presbyterian, Jackson, when we were first married. Of course, it was originally written in German and later translated into English. I am so thankful we had the opportunity to sing it in English, as these words have continued to wash over me, giving me renewed hope year after year. The words have such power because they were taken straight from the Bible. At the time we sang it, I had no idea how I would cling to these Scriptures for hope years later. The lyrics are composed of Scriptures about the brevity of this life and about the resurrection.

These are some of my favorite scriptures included in this work:

They that sow in tears shall reap in joy. (Psalm 126:5 KJV)

For all flesh is as grass, and all the glory of man as the flower of grass. (1 Peter 1:24 KJV)

But the word of the Lord endureth forever. (1 Peter 1:25 KJV)

And the ransomed of the Lord shall return, and come to Zion with songs and everlasting joy upon their heads; they shall obtain joy and gladness, and sorrow and sighing shall flee away. (Isaiah 35:10 KJV)

Lord, make me to know mine end, and the measure of my days, what it is: that I may know how frail I am. Behold, thou hast made my days as an handbreadth; and mine age is as nothing before thee... And now, Lord, what wait I for? My hope is in thee. (Psalm 39:4–7 KJV)

But the souls of the righteous are in the hand of God, and there shall no torment touch them. (Song of Solomon 3:1 KJV)

How amiable are thy tabernacles, O Lord of hosts! My soul longeth, yea, even fainteth for the courts of the Lord; my heart and my flesh crieth out for the living God. Blessed are they that dwell in thy house; they will be still praising thee. (Psalm 84:1, 2, 4 KJV)

And ye now therefore have sorrow; but I will see you again, and your heart shall rejoice, and your joy no man taketh from you. (John 16:22 KJV)

For here have we no continuing city, but we seek one to come. (Hebrews 13:14 KJV)

Thou art worthy, O Lord, to receive glory and honour and power; for thou hast created all things, and for thy pleasure they are and were created. (Revelation 4:11 KJV)

And of course, the beautiful description of the resurrection from 1 Corinthians 15:

We shall not all sleep, but we shall all be changed, in a moment, in the twinkling of an eye, at the last trumpet. (1 Corinthians 15:51–52 ESV)

Nowadays I do still decorate for Christmas, but I didn't want to do much for a few years. I have gradually added more decorations to the house because my children, especially Caleb, love them. And maybe it's a way to shake my fist at the enemy, to let him know that he won't win. We will continue to celebrate Christmas because of what it truly means. It is not about the stuff and lots of extended family being together, and it's not about traditions. It is about our God, who came down to dwell with us. He came to burst through our darkness and to bring light and hope. He came to suffer in a way that we never will; he came as our substitute.

There are so many sad and horrific things that happen in this broken world, and we can be tempted to think that God doesn't care, that he is asleep, or that he throws his hands up in the air in defeat. None of this is true.

Henry Wadsworth Longfellow captures this so beautifully in his 1863 poem, "Christmas Bells." Written during the Civil War, it begins with despair that the bells are mocking the song of "peace on earth, goodwill to men." Toward the end of the poem, the bells bring renewed hope. The group Casting Crowns put Longfellow's words to a new tune in "I Heard the Bells on Christmas Day." Emily's high school choir, Vision, sang this during the school's Christmas chapel several times, and it moves me to tears every time I hear it. This past Christmas, when we were skiing and surrounded by the beautiful snow and mountains of Colorado, I found myself pondering these words over and over.

> And in despair I bowed my head;
> "There is no peace on earth," I said:
> For hate is strong,
> And mocks the song
> Of peace on earth, good-will to men!"
>
> Then pealed the bells more loud and deep:
> "God is not dead; nor doth He sleep!
> The Wrong shall fail,
> The Right prevail,
> With peace on earth, good-will to men."
>
> (Henry Wadsworth Longfellow, "Christmas Bells")

Amazing and true words! *God is not dead; nor doth he sleep!*

Afterword

In the years since the tragedies, I continue to be amazed that we are still here and able to carry on with daily life. I know I should not be surprised, since God's Word is pregnant with promises that he will sustain his people and that he will never leave us.

I still struggle with doubt. Depression still rears its ugly head occasionally, but I have learned to recognize it as one of his ways of reminding me of my dependence on him. Heaven looks sweeter with every passing day.

I miss my mom and Will's mom every day. When I just want a momma to talk to, or when I want to share something my kids have done, even with the passage of time, I still have the urge to pick up the phone and call them. I really miss not being able to call them.

Will continues to practice medicine. He has always had great compassion for his patients, but it has grown deeper after all he has suffered.

About a year after my mom died, Dad began to date. Soon he met Sissy, and they were married. They are so happy together, and we are so happy for them!

Emily has started college. She has seen so much suffering and experienced so much heartache in her young life. In the days leading up to leaving home for her freshman year, she grew quieter and quieter, anticipating this major life change. As the six of us loaded the van and Emily's car the night before leaving, she began to sob in the driveway. The boys and Will and I all surrounded her in a huge embrace as she continued to sob. Eventually, Will and the boys went into the house, leaving just the two of us standing in front of the house.

I pulled her into my arms. Through heavy sobbing, she said, "Mom, I'm so afraid something will happen to y'all when I'm not here." I said, "Oh, sweetie, I know. Something could happen when we're all here together too. All we can do is trust that God will be with us whatever happens." I was so thankful she was able to voice her fears.

William and Luke, the little boys who used to curl up next to Mom in her bed to watch movies, or snuggle in her lap in her wheelchair, are now young men. William has gone off to college, and Luke is in high school. Caleb, who as a baby used to pull up on Mom's wheelchair before he could walk, will be headed to high school soon. He has such a sweet compassion for those who are suffering or in need.

*****

When these tragedies struck our family, I never believed that we would truly be able to live joyfully and thrive. But as God often does, he has surprised me. As painful as it is, he grows our faith in seasons of loss and suffering. He uses it to increase our longing for him and for heaven. He has brought my heart to a place where I can read scripture such as Psalms 27:13–14 and say that it is true. It says, "I believe that I shall look upon the goodness of the Lord in the land of the living! Wait for the Lord; be strong, and let your heart take courage; wait for the Lord!" (ESV).

I believe the "goodness of the Lord" can be what we see as temporal blessings, but I have come to understand that it is ultimately being in fellowship with Jesus. It is him and his presence with us throughout all of life, and he is trustworthy.

In spite of suffering, uncertainties, and doubts, I am confident of what the final outcome will be. Through his death and resurrection, Jesus secured my final home in heaven with him. Not only that, but until then, I can continue to live with the confidence that he loves me and he is sovereign. This does not mean that life will be easy. It does mean that he will always be with me, whether I am in the valley or on the mountaintop. In Matthew 28:20, Jesus says, "And surely I am with you always, to the very end of the age" (NIV).

Jesus says, "Yes, I am coming soon," in Revelation 22:20. The verse continues, "Amen. Come, Lord Jesus" (Revelation 22:20 NIV). As Will's mother wrote, it's "not much longer now!"

Bibliography

Anderson, Reggie with Jennifer Schuchmann. *Appointments with Heaven: The True Story of a Country Doctor's Healing Encounters with the Hereafter.* Tyndale, 2013.

Holy Bible. Quoted verses taken from New International Version, English Standard Version, and King James Version, as noted.

Keller, Timothy. *Walking with God through Pain and Suffering.* New York: Penguin Group, 2013.

Lloyd-Jones, Sally. *The Jesus Storybook Bible.* Grand Rapids, Michigan: Zondervan, 2007.

———*Thoughts to Make your Heart Sing.* Grand Rapids, Michigan: Zondervan, 2012.

Longfellow, Henry Wadsworth. "Christmas Bells." 1864.

Owens, Stephen with Ken Abraham. *Set Free: Discover Forgiveness amidst Murder and Betrayal.* Nashville, Tennessee: B&H Publishing Group, 2013.

Spurgeon, Charles H. *Morning and Evening.* Hendrickson Publishers, Inc., 1991.

Tada, Joni Eareckson and Steven Estes. *When God Weeps: Why Our Sufferings Matter to the Almighty.* Grand Rapids, Michigan: Zondervan, 1997.

Tada, Joni Eareckson and Bobbie Wolgemuth. *Hymns for a Kid's Heart, Volume One.* Wheaton, Illinois: Crossway Books, 2003.

———*Hymns for a Kid's Heart, Volume Two.* Wheaton, Illinois: Crossway Books, 2004.

Trinity Hymnal. Suwanee, Georgia: Great Commission Publications, Inc., 1990.

Our parents were such good friends. L to R—Bill and
Susan Mayfield, Doug and Lynn Wheeler, 1997.

Julie and Lynn, on Will and Julie's
wedding day, June 28, 1997.

September 23, 1999. Bill, Lynn, Doug, and Susan
surrounding Will, Julie, and baby Emily.

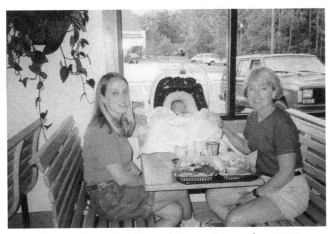

Julie, newborn Emily, and Lynn, September 1999.

Three generations. L to R—Will, William,
and Bill Mayfield in 2002.

William and Emily enjoying donuts with
Gram and Grandpop, 2003.

All four grandparents helping us move
to Cincinnati, Summer 2003.

Mom (Lynn) with Emily, Luke, and
William, October 2004.

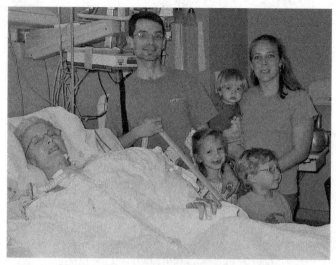

Visiting Lynn in the hospital in April of
2006, just four months post-injury.

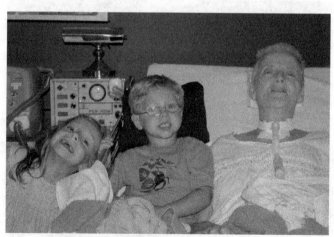

Emily and William watching a movie
with Gram, June 2006.

Lynn meeting Joni Eareckson Tada for the first
time. September 2006, nine months post-injury.

Emily and Luke playing piano with Grandmother
(Susan Mayfield), Christmas 2006.

Will and Julie's family visiting Doug
and Lynn in January of 2007.

Will's parents (Bill and Susan) on vacation in the
mountains with Will and Julie's family, September 2007.

Radnor Lake with Will's parents, February, 2008.

Being silly with Grandmother (Susan), 2008.

Boys hugging Pop goodbye, 2008.

Emily and Grandmother enjoying a visit on
the porch in Jackson, January, 2009.

Caleb blowing a dandelion for Gram, March 2009.

William helping to load Gram into her van, March 2009.

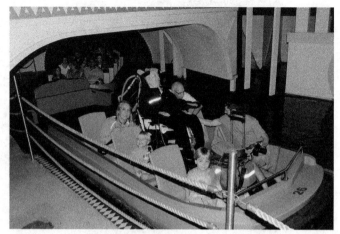

January 2011, Lynn on It's a Small
World at Walt Disney World.

William and Pop (Bill) enjoying a
game of chess, Summer 2012.

Enjoying a visit with Will's parents,
Bill and Susan, Summer 2012.

Back row L to R—Doug, Bill, Susan, Emily. Front
row L to R—William, Luke, Lynn, and Caleb. August
2013, only eight months before the shooting.

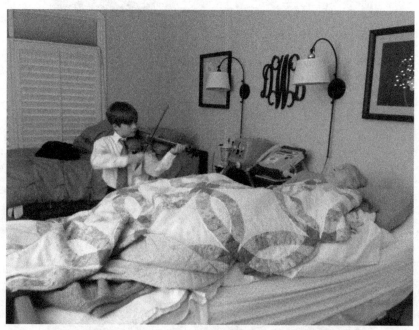

Luke playing violin for Gram, October 2015.

October 31, 2015, Julie's family trick-or-treating
at Gram's bedside. She died a month later.

About the Author

Julie Mayfield lives in Nashville, Tennessee, with her husband, Will, and their four children, Emily, William, Luke, and Caleb. A former elementary teacher, Julie serves as a deaconess at Christ Presbyterian Church in Nashville. She enjoys hiking, music, serving in disability ministry, and making memories with her family at theme parks.